HOW GOVERNMENT *REALLY* WORKS

A field guide to bureaucracies in Canada

HOW GOVERNMENT REALLY WORKS

A field guide to bureaucracies
in Canada

HOW GOVERNMENT *REALLY* WORKS

A field guide to bureaucracies in Canada

JANE ALLT AND ANGELA POIRIER

Formac Publishing Company Limited
Halifax

We dedicate this book to all the hard-working bureaucrats serving the public interest and especially to the leaders who inspired us — some of whom are referenced in this book.

Formac Publishing Company Limited recognizes the support of the Province of Nova Scotia through Film and Creative Industries Nova Scotia. We are pleased to work in partnership with the Province of Nova Scotia to develop and promote our creative industries for the benefit of all Nova Scotians. We acknowledge the support of the Canada Council for the Arts which last year invested $157 million to bring the arts to Canadians throughout the country.

Cover design: Tyler Cleroux
Cover images: Shutterstock

Library and Archives Canada Cataloguing in Publication

Title: How government really works : a field guide to bureaucracies in Canada / Jane Allt and Angela Poirier.
Names: Allt, Jane, author. | Poirier, Angela, author.
Description: Includes bibliographical references and index.
Identifiers: Canadiana (print) 20200259989 | Canadiana (ebook) 2020026026X | ISBN 9781459506282 (softcover) | ISBN 9781459506299 (EPUB)
Subjects: LCSH: Bureaucracy—Canada. | LCSH: Civil service—Canada.
Classification: LCC JL108 .A37 2020 | DDC 352.6/30971—dc23

Formac Publishing Company Limited
5502 Atlantic Street
Halifax, Nova Scotia, Canada
B3H 1G4
www.formac.ca

Printed and bound in Canada.

CONTENTS

CONTENTS

FOREWORD

THE HONOURABLE JOCELYNE BOURGON, P.C., O.C.

Public policy practitioners and scholars in the 21st century have become acutely aware of the widening gap between the theory and practice of public administration. One of the most important ways to bridge this gap is to capture the learning journeys and experiences of public sector leaders. Angela and Jane, bringing 60 years of combined service with the Nova Scotia government, make a rich contribution by broadening the conversation on the structure and culture of government.

People working in government today are serving in an environment characterized by a high level of complexity, uncertainty, volatility and unpredictability. This book serves as a guide for aspiring civil servants, current civil servants, elected officials and students of public policy/administration to successfully navigate the complex terrains of serving in government today. Merging practical experience and advice, the authors shine a light on the dynamics of serving the collective interest.

An important insight from the book is that public interest is a collective enterprise that involves governments, citizens and many other actors coming together to invent solutions to complex and intractable problems that stem from living in society. Public sector leaders use the authority of the state as a lever to steer society through a process of change, harness the collective power of society, influence behaviours and transform the relationship between the public, private and civic spheres of life. This is often a delicate balancing act. As in the past, the state must be able to govern and the public apparatus must be able to get things done. But, more than ever, government must nurture the capacity to invent solutions and to build the adaptive capacity and the resilience of society.

There is more to the role of civil servants than to manage publicly funded programs and provide public services. Civil servants serve a public purpose. They are value creators in society. Guided by public service values such as integrity, neutrality and accountability, civil servants support the state's ultimate responsibility as the "guardian of the public good." At the most fundamental level, this is what makes the public sector unique and most valuable for society and what gives meaning to government decisions and actions.

Another vital contribution of this book is that it highlights the importance of collaboration across government systems. Silos and hierarchies are key characteristics of bureaucratic organizations. Although they are useful for the purposes of accountability, they often pose a barrier to active collaboration, experimentation and innovation. Leveraging positive relationships and building collaborative approaches can counter agency-centric tendencies and generate results of higher public value at a lower overall cost to society. However, collaboration does not happen by accident. Public sector leaders must take deliberate steps to promote collaboration and exercise influence over a vast ecosystem of interdependent relationships. They must reconcile their vertical accountability for delegated authority with the need to operate through vast networks to achieve shared and collective results. Despite efforts to encourage evidence-based decision making, governments often have to make decisions with imperfect knowledge and unknown impacts. As guardians of the public good, they are called upon to make difficult decisions in order to propel society forward. This is not an easy task.

Reading this book will give you practical insights on how to navigate public organizations and make a difference in society.

JOCELYNE BOURGON is President of Public Governance International (PGI) and President Emerita of the Canada School of Public Service. She has a distinguished career of public service, including serving as deputy minister of several major federal government departments, Secretary to the Cabinet for federal-provincial relations, and later as Clerk of the Privy Council and Secretary to Cabinet. She is a Member of the Order of Canada and a Knight of the National Order of Merit of the Republic of France. She has published extensively on the subject of public administration and is the author of A New Synthesis of Public Administration: Serving in the 21st Century *(2011) and* The New Synthesis of Public Administration Fieldbook *(2017).*

INTRODUCTION

Should you wonder why we would write a book about bureaucrats, the answer is simple: we want to lift the veil on the world of bureaucracy and share the challenges of working in a politically charged environment.

When we started this journey, we thought politicians and the public got enough airtime on this topic, and it was about time someone shared the bureaucrat's playbook to ensure all voices were heard.

As fate would have it, we wrapped up the first draft of this book just before the world got sideswiped by COVID-19. The irony is not lost on us, as the premise of this book is that bureaucrats play a critical role in the health and well-being of citizens. We know first-hand that pandemic planning was on the radar for bureaucrats across the country for a long time and is an ongoing activity within bureaucracies. Knowing this has provided us with comfort during these uncertain times.

Many bureaucrats were front and centre in the fight to control the spread of the virus, secure needed goods and services to protect essential workers, deliver emergency services, restructure and increase the capacity of the health system to respond to the crisis and to introduce, as well as administer, economic lifelines to citizens and businesses alike.

Like us, friends and neighbours experienced a void in the many public services that were no longer available — from public education and elective health services to libraries, museums, recreation and parks. These programs and services delivered by public servants add significant value to our quality of life. We believe they have often been taken for granted and their absence may make people more appreciative of the public goods they have enjoyed.

Throughout these pages you will find our reflections on the bureaucracy in place to deliver and guard the many programs and services of Canada's social welfare economy. And while much of the material represents governments as usual, the premise of this book is more important than ever before in light of the COVID-19 pandemic.

We share the good, the bad and the ugly when it comes to serving elected officials. And we also share plenty of lessons learned on how bureaucrats navigate the inherently complex and sometimes dysfunctional environment that is always under the critical eye of the opposition and the general public.

We have spent our careers working in Nova Scotia. That NS was the first British colony to win responsible government back in 1848 was regularly mentioned during our tenure. It sparked an element of pride to know the province we served also served as the cradle of parliamentary accountability in the country.

Our federation has come a long way since that time, with bureaucrats at national, provincial and local levels of government enacting laws and delivering programs and services within the confines of "geographical boundaries, constitutional status, and particular powers and jurisdictions."[1]

Despite being a much-maligned profession, bureaucrats are essential in a democracy. They are the people who make governments work. They are the sober second thought politicians need to hear, especially when partisan behaviours may not be in the public interest. One only has to consider the experience of Donald Trump's presidency, wherein many people saw bureaucrats as ethical, hard-working, loyal individuals doing their best to counter the self-interest of the leadership and protect the wealth and well-being of all citizens.

Not to belabour the point — okay, maybe we will a little — but consider these words shared with us from Doug Keefe, a long-serving and respected provincial bureaucrat who inspired us as a leader and "truth to power" broker:

> It's trite but true that a professional public service is the flywheel of democracy and an institution crucial to good public administration. Its role is to provide competency and continuity to public affairs, and stability, expertise, and a voice of moderation to the internal deliberations of government. The members of the governing party have the means of getting their voices heard. At its best the public service reminds ministers of the views of the 'outs' — the people who aren't supporters of the party in power — and the 'down and out's' of society more generally.

With that lofty role, one could reasonably expect some respect. But alas, that is not the case. Part of our motivation for writing this book comes from the image problems bureaucrats throughout the country endure. While many professions face negativity, the level and the amount of criticism directed towards bureaucrats can be disheartening. We hope to build the bridge to empathy for bureaucrats, many of whom dedicate their careers to providing goods and services to citizens.

Consider the results of an informal survey, which is not statistically sound, but telling nonetheless. We asked a number of people to tell us what first comes to their mind when they hear the word "bureaucrat." While there were a few positive comments smattered throughout their responses, the vast majority were negative, as the following list shows. Please keep in mind; these comments came from friends — the people who love us and who we expected would say nice things because we were bureaucrats:

- Person who sits at a desk shuffling papers from side to side;
- Like the lyrics from an old song: bend me, shape me, anyway you

want me. I figure that a bureaucrat just becomes what the politicians of the day want;

- Meddler;
- Paid naysayer;
- Useless helpers;
- Well-paid mouthpieces;
- Political puppets;
- Vindictive;
- People who may want to help but lack the backbone to do so;
- One who works by fixed routine, seldom exercising intelligent judgement; and
- Generally seen as lacklustre, who at the same time want efficiency and who are usually associated with big things like the civil service and wads of paperwork. Though generally such types don't exist anymore, the stereotypical bureaucrat's favourite colour is brown of some variety and enjoys sucking the life out of stuff by involving lots of forms and not doing a lot themselves by delegating respon- sibilities, yet retaining their power. Bureaucracy is thus a negative thing and to be avoided at all costs.

We admit we've run into our share of the bureaucratic archetypes, including the scattered do-gooder; the pass-the-bucker; the hyper- vigilant protector of the public good; and the nervous risk-averter, but these archetypes can be found in any large organization. However, most of the colleagues we worked with — in our home province and across the country — were dedicated and hardworking civil servants who identified, developed and delivered the goods and services that keep our society running.

This may sound self-serving because we were career civil servants and between us spent 60 years working for a provincial government. One of us joined when you could simply walk in the door of a department, be greeted by a secretary, meet the person hiring and start the job the next day. The other joined years later and went through a competitive interview process. But that didn't stop *Frank Magazine* from suggesting she was a political hire because of a long-ago connection to the riding of the minister who led the department at the time.

Together we worked in almost every aspect of provincial government responsibility, changed our careers many times and held roles where we served as analysts, facilitators, managers, advisors, leaders, mediators and even spin doctors.

We both have master's degrees in public administration from Dalhousie University. It was during our studies that we first contemplated writing a book about bureaucrats. We learned a great deal in our courses, but often felt the theories associated with public administration were a far cry from the realities of working in government. We could relate to the notion that civil servants across the country sometimes lead lives of quiet collusion because we navigated many dysfunctions within the system that were never openly discussed.

What finally prompted us to put "pen to paper" was a rather innocuous incident involving a tick-box recognition card designed by the agency responsible for Nova Scotia's public servants and distributed to managers to use with their employees. Several colleagues were dismayed that a mass-produced card declaring "official acknowledgement of gratitude" for a "check all that apply" list of actions, sentiments and impacts would be viewed as a good idea. Most are aware that recognition should be geared towards an individual and their needs and wants, and an impersonal generic card that takes less than five seconds to tick off doesn't cut it. Given all the heat bureaucrats take on a daily basis, we thought they — and we — deserved better.

To be clear, we're not trying to denigrate the people who thought the card was a good idea. We think the attempt speaks to the impersonal relationships awash in the civil service, as so many people are focused on task.

We're going to share our take on those tasks, and you'll see we've supplemented our own knowledge with insights from people who have occupied senior roles within government. We've also mined our academic lessons on public administration and included a "Case in Point" section, where we test some of the concepts explored in the chapters. We hope you'll appreciate our all-important "Talking Points."

If you're pressed for time or need a 30-second sound bite about lessons to be gleaned from said chapters, check out this section in each chapter. Bureaucrats regularly produce talking points for politicians to deliver to media and to respond to questions in the "house." And there are additional insights from others in a "Don't take our word for it" section, which reinforces points made in the chapter.

Our definition of bureaucrats for the purposes of this book are civil servants hired based on merit and working in or from government offices throughout the land — be they program officers, administrators, researchers, analysts, managers, supervisors or leaders. These employees are also often referred to as "public servants," although that term can encompass those elected or appointed to positions.

Given this book is about government, you'll also find many references to that term. Unless otherwise indicated, when we refer to "government," we are including both elected officials and civil servants.

Some of the examples we use do not always show government in the best light. Our intention is not to disparage or point fingers, but rather to illustrate some of the challenging situations we faced. We recognize that everyone's experiences are different.

Despite a chorus of public criticism that bureaucrats don't do enough or are ineffective, we beg to differ. We encourage anybody with an interest in, or who interacts with, bureaucracy to turn the page and read on. This includes employees, politicians, union leaders, students in disciplines such as public administration, political science and law, as well as organizations that deal with or rub up against a bureaucracy.

One last caveat: much of what we describe in the following pages uses Nova Scotia as the launching pad for discussing features of the bureaucracy and tasks performed. The broad strokes of what happens in the NS bureaucracy is similar, if not identical, across the country, but we highlight the differences when warranted. While our experience comes from provincial jurisdiction, we believe what you'll read is applicable to all levels of government.

Chapter 1

HOUSE OF CARDS

*"The Prime Minister holds power. Ministers have
responsibility. Fortunately, the civil service retains control."*

— Sir Humphrey Appleby, *Yes Minister*

IN THIS CHAPTER:
- Guardian of the Public Good
- Politicians and Bureaucrats
- Hierarchy
- Checkmate — Political Controls That Keep Bureaucrats in Check
- Back at You — Bureaucratic Controls That Keep Politicians in Check

We struggled with where to start this behind-the-scenes look at the world of bureaucracy, as this beleaguered system of administration is daunting and plagued by stereotypes and negative perceptions. Our publisher didn't help with our struggle; he rolled his eyes and let out a sigh when we told him we settled on explaining the belly of the beast, including the bureaucrat's role, for the first chapter.

Maybe you just let out a sigh, too. And that's okay. We admit it does not sound exciting, but we promise to keep it light and brief. We're making the case that it's worth your time to read our take on the monolith of government structure, including the principles that govern a bureaucrat's work life, because their actions affect your life, too. At the very least, you may get a better idea of where to point fingers when criticizing something government has done. More significantly, we hope you will gain a better appreciation of the critical role bureaucrats play in protecting democratic institutions and public services against partisan or personal interests.

We knew little about government structure until we found ourselves in the thick of it, but as we learned about the beast, it helped us to recognize and explain what was right and wrong with the government workplace.

For starters, we'll explore government's role as guardian of the public good, and we'll follow that with a look at the structural features and principles that shape how bureaucrats deliver those goods. We'll conclude with some thoughts on controls that keep government players in check. This information will lay the foundation for many of the issues we explore in the chapters that follow.

We understand that democracy has its share of challenges, but it's worth quoting Winston Churchill: "No one pretends that democracy is perfect or all-wise. Indeed, it has been said that democracy is the worst form of government except for all those other forms that have been tried from time to time …"[1]

Of course, there is a price to pay for our country-wide system, and that includes the cost of bureaucracy. For context, bear with us as we briefly revisit the origin of the term, which was coined in the mid-18th century by a French economist and — no surprise — it was first used pejoratively. A quick online search will tell you by the mid-19th century, the word was used neutrally and regarded as a distinct form of management, often subservient to a monarchy. In the 1920s, the definition was expanded by German sociologist Max Weber to include any system of administration conducted by trained professionals, according to fixed rules. We expect that last part rings true to you, because you've likely encountered many of those rules when dealing with government. We know we have.

Fast-forward decades, and we are now in an era where many Canadians view bureaucrats as a drain on society and a target for reduction by the public and elected officials. We aren't going to argue the merits of that position, but we can unequivocally claim that public service spending has significant benefits for citizens.

It is easier to recognize the value of public services in an emergency, including the care extended by paramedics, the critical responses from fire and police services and the massive mobilization of government services during the pandemic in 2020. But it is harder to distinguish and appreciate public service benefits as we go about our daily lives. For most of us, those benefits started with prenatal health care — including the recording of our birth. The benefits continued as we grew up, including tapping into educational and public health services and enjoying numerous recreational and cultural activities within our communities. Those benefits also extended into our workplaces — from labour laws governing wages, benefits and occupational health and safety, to the transportation networks we used to get to those jobs. Staying true to form, these benefits help in our later years through programs such as Seniors' Pharmacare and the distribution of pension benefits.

Guardian of the Public Good

What we described is the tip of the iceberg when it comes to the services citizens receive from government. In some cases, we hope we won't use the services, but they ensure public safety and lawful governance, such as correctional services and public prosecution services, as well as criminal and civil court processes. We're thankful when we don't need others, such as income assistance, disability supports and long-term care; although, we are glad they are in place for those who do need them. Other services are critical to our environment and economy, including the management of natural resources and protection of the environment.

Bureaucrats throughout the country will recognize the following three key principles that guide the work civil servants undertake to guard and deliver the public goods society enjoys. We — like many of our former colleagues — took those principles seriously.

1. No party favours

The first principle centres on non-partisanship, which requires bureaucrats to serve the government of the day with impartiality, no matter what the party's ideology and without falling prey to party favours.

Key tenants of non-partisanship include speaking truth to power, but also loyalty in carrying out the tasks of those who hold the power.

As Keefe explained, the professional civil service "gives confidential advice to, and carries out lawful instructions of, the government of the day. When we say the public service is loyal to the government, this — not partisanship — is what we mean. So, public servants should be non-partisan but they cannot be politically naïve since it is their duty to serve the current administration to the best of their abilities, while at the same time maintaining confidence in the public and amongst those who may one day govern. The path of loyalty and neutrality is hard to tread in government since the path is notional and the countryside rugged."

Like many bureaucrats, we struggled along that path more than a few times when we thought decisions being made by elected officials were ill advised. But we also knew that unless it was unlawful, there was little we could do and carried out the wishes of the governing party as we were required.

2. Making the case
This brings us to the second principle that centres on evidence. Bureaucrats are expected to provide advice to decision makers that is grounded in research and analysis. Despite the stereotypes, for the most part, bureaucrats are competent, well-educated in their chosen field and work hard to generate evidence for decision making. Of course, that doesn't mean elected officials always take the advice, resulting in decisions that can be contrary to the evidence presented. On more than one occasion, we had to bite our tongues when politicians ignored evidence that did not align with partisan or ideological goals. In those cases, we knew politicians questioned our loyalty or thought we were being obstructionists. But that is a price one pays for speaking truth to power.

3. Fair play
The third key principle can be summed up as fair play. It requires bureaucrats to assess recommended actions in the context of human rights, public interest and the rule of law. Undertaking that work

requires significant time and effort, and it's why we think bureaucrats are often accused of stalling or of being overly cautious.

You'll read about these principles in practice in the chapters that follow, but we're now going to turn our attention to where bureaucrats reside within the overall structure of government.

Politicians and Bureaucrats

When people bandy about the term "government," they often group bureaucrats in with elected officials, especially if they're angry about a government action or decision. Unlike politicians, bureaucrats are unelected and hired through fair competition. For the most part, they work in departments for which ministers of an elected party are ultimately accountable.

Departments are sometimes referred to as silos — a key feature of government structure — because the people working there focus on and understand a relatively narrow slice of an area, issue, service or population. As you may know, silos are used on farms to store various types of grain and prevent them from mixing. In a government's case, the term is often used derogatorily to describe the lack of information that flows between departments.

That lack of information flow is one of the reasons why we often heard cries to eliminate departments, with many suggesting silos are ill-suited to deal with complex, multi-faceted issues that require expertise and responsibilities from across the system. This is especially pronounced in the federal government, given its wide geographical spread and the size of its civil service.

However, silos are essential for public accountability because they focus power and duty on one person — namely the minister responsible for each department. Those ministers make up the cabinet, which is collectively accountable to the legislature and thus to the public, for the overall performance of the government. For additional clarity, a provincial cabinet "typically determines government priorities, sets the levels of taxation and spending, makes key appointments and oversees the administration of government departments. The size of a provincial cabinet varies in proportion to the size of the particular province. Prince Edward Island, for example, tends to have around 10–15 cabinet ministers, while Ontario's cabinet averages around 25–30 ministers."[2]

On a personal level, if you have a beef with government, a little digging should uncover the minister responsible for whatever issue ails you. If you write to that minister, they are obliged to respond. Mind you, the response may be a deflection or an obfuscation. We can attest to that because we were tasked with drafting many responses over the years, and we have a lot more to say about the process in our last chapter on communications.

Structures and restructuring in government

You may have envisioned a silo as a strong, immobile structure. However, in the context of government, they can be and are often torn down, renovated or built at the whim of the governing party. This usually happens following the election of a new government, and our experience suggests most restructuring has little to do with improving government functions. Rather, it is a tool government sometimes uses to show they are doing something when they don't know what to do. We compared restructuring to fashion trends. You know — wait long enough and what was old will be new again.

One of us started out in the Department of Mines and Energy decades ago. Over the years, many name changes and restructures followed, and at the time of writing this book, the department name was back to where it started, with a flip to energy and mines. Given the specialized work, many of the same people who were there under the mines and energy title are still there, undoubtedly shaking their heads and questioning the purpose and sense of all the name changes.

While we served, departments with an economic focus were particularly prone to meddling because some elected officials thought they could direct the economy. Perhaps politicians also feel safer fiddling with them as the public rarely puts up a fuss about changes to less public-facing departments, such as business and tourism portfolios. When politicians mess with departments like health, community services or education, they are often met with public outrage; unions threatening to strike or slow services down; and specialists working in those fields threatening to quit. This is unfortunate as it is often these large, complex, high-profile departments that need to be shaken up to address new challenges.

Tinkering with any department results in angst and discontentment. Consider the case of a relatively senior employee, who had been through four restructures in about eight years. He started to refer to human resources employees as "the undertakers of the world" because those individuals were constantly delivering difficult news about changes that would negatively impact people in the department. After the fourth restructure and a request by a human resources employee for a few minutes of his time, he assumed the worst and immediately said, "If you've come to offer me another f----ing opportunity, I'm done, I just can't do it anymore."

We also recall another instance, wherein human resources employees spent months implementing a significant restructure that had huge impacts on employees, including layoffs and reassignments. The ground had not even stopped shaking under these employees' feet when a deputy minister called a human resources director at home to let her know they would be making an announcement the next day about yet another staff reorganization.

We're not suggesting that change isn't good and necessary. However, there is a downside if the change is simply to *imply* something is being done. Bureaucrats often pay the price for such tinkering because restructuring usually comes with layoffs. Taxpayers pay a price, too, as despite what politicians say, these changes come with a hefty price tag.

Politicians often justify restructuring by telling the public changes will increase efficiencies and save money. We beg to differ. Most changes we lived through came with significant costs, including rebranding everything from stationary and door signs to vehicles and uniforms. The employees left behind were often stressed; that translated into lost productivity. In extreme cases, individuals succumbed to the uncertainty and tapped into the health-care system, which obviously comes with a cost. And while people were laid off, their work didn't disappear. Those gaps eventually became apparent, as remaining employees were not able to keep up with the tasks. Thus, new positions were advertised and eventually refilled, therefore reducing any supposed savings achieved from the round of layoffs announced as part of the restructuring.

Hierarchy

With that overview of silos behind us, we're now going to look at another dominant structural feature in government. It should come as no surprise that hierarchy looms large in federal, provincial and municipal bureaucracies — as it does in any large organization.

Within government structures, there are layers upon layers of bureaucrats — some far removed from those who are doing the work — who scrutinize, challenge and advance the work of those below them. In theory, hierarchy is meant to ensure clear and transparent roles and responsibilities. In reality, it can easily lead to impersonal and painfully slow services for citizens and bureaucrats alike.

There is no question that government structure is management heavy, and when bureaucrats want to move up the chain of command, there are many titles to pursue. Starting at the top — in Nova Scotia and elsewhere, you can find senior deputy ministers, deputy ministers, associate deputies and assistant deputies, as well as strategic advisors to these senior leaders. After this group, you'll find senior executive directors, executive directors, directors, managers, supervisors and team leads. As you move down the chain, there are senior analysts and analysts, senior researchers and researchers, senior officers and officers — you get the point. These titles are from the provincial level of bureaucracies; at the federal level, the titles tend to sound loftier with "regional" often added to the various management layers.

Because it can be difficult to figure out who is who in the hierarchy, anybody who deals with or works in bureaucracy should keep a cheat-sheet to track who to impress and who to avoid. Lobbyists and advocates may want to make it a point to get to know the people below the minister and deputy minister — these people can slow things down or speed things up. We'll explore why later in this chapter.

Bureaucrats should also be wary of getting too cozy with anybody who is political. They shouldn't ride the coattails of those who are the chosen ones at any given time, because people in those positions often fall out of favour quickly, taking others with them. One of us was recruited to join the "in-crowd" at a central agency. We were warned that if we refused, it would not look good for our career progression. Thankfully, we didn't take the bait. Soon after, it did not take long for that leader to fall out of grace. Many reputations were forever tarnished because of their connection to her.

In theory, a bureaucrat's marching orders come from a deputy minister, who gets their marching orders from a minister. A minister supposedly receives marching orders from the electorate. However, we witnessed a significant increase in orders coming from political handlers, who got their orders from the premier's office. One would expect a high level of political scrutiny on the big-ticket items, such as new laws or larger spending commitments, but towards the end of our careers, even the most innocuous actions had to be sanctioned by central control. We understood this was happening in various degrees in bureaucracies throughout the country. Some claim the practice took off under former Prime Minister Stephen Harper, and many leaders followed suit.

Central agencies

One last note about structure concerns the central agencies found within provincial bureaucracies, where one will find bureaucrats working alongside political staff. These central agencies tend to focus on areas such as policy, treasury and communications. Regulatory affairs were added to the mix in Nova Scotia towards the end of our careers. These agencies have many rules, procedures and directives bureaucrats must follow. We expect many bureaucrats throughout the land will nod in agreement that employees in these departments tend to introduce themselves as "the ones who are here to help." But we, like many other colleagues, soon learned to greet many of these helpers with caution and dread. They wanted to be of assistance, but their role was to scrutinize our work, which often involved delving into areas where they were not specialists with the desire to insert their own biases or to act on political will.

We recall an instance where a central policy shop used its muscle to force the bureaucracy to do its bidding. A powerful lobby group demanded government change an act that would give them specific authorities over others. We argued that it would be unwise for government to delegate its authority to a third party for which it did not control. Research had shown that no other jurisdiction had done what was requested. We made the case in countless submissions and kept getting push back from the scrutinizers who asked us whether we considered this or that. Just when we thought we satisfied all questions, our recommendation was not accepted. It was back to the drawing board, where we were told to recommend the course of action demanded by the lobby group. To add insult to injury, we were told not to categorize them as a lobby group in the reworked paperwork.

Central government agencies have their own layers of bureaucratic requirements, including an insatiable demand for filling out templates specific to whatever permission was being sought — whether that was a spending item; a policy position; a procurement requirement; or planned communications. We found it ironic that while red tape reduction was and is an especially appealing area of focus for new governments, they rarely applied that thinking internally. In our experience, every new government introduced more paperwork requirements, continually adding layers of red tape onto departments. We know bureaucrats in NS weren't the only ones throughout the country who faced increasing paper burdens.

Checkmate — Political Controls That Keep Bureaucrats in Check

Red tape is one of the ways that politicians corral the work of the bureaucracy, which brings us to a discussion of power, control and the dance that goes on daily between elected officials and the bureaucrats who serve. Elected leaders keep bureaucrats in check through a variety of measures.

1. Do as I say

First and foremost, bureaucrats are beholden to elected leaders. As a former colleague bluntly said: politicians are elected, bureaucrats are not. They call the shots. She also had this advice for bureaucrats: "if you don't like those terms or want that role, go out and get yourself elected so you can be the boss, or find another job."

Any authority bureaucrats do have is specifically delegated through legislation and ultimately controlled by politicians. Ministers remain responsible and accountable for all decisions made within departments, although some won't hesitate to throw bureaucrats under the bus when the news is bad. And when they do, the authority of elected officials over the public service is undermined. As Keefe says, "I found myself saying to a minister on one occasion, 'If you're going to blame me publicly for the decision, I'm going to make it.'"

It is also worth noting the following observation: "In theory, cabinet ministers are individually responsible for their departments and collectively responsible for government policies. In practice, however, provincial premiers tend to dominate provincial cabinets. The premier is the effective head of the provincial government, and is equivalent to the federal prime minister. Like their federal counterpart, provincial premiers have the power to appoint and dismiss cabinet ministers. This, in turn, provides them with considerable power to direct cabinet priorities and policies, as well as the general operation of government. A premier may choose cabinet ministers that demonstrate loyalty and/or reflect his/her own political point of view and may dismiss ministers that fail to tow the premier's line."[3]

2. Setting the agenda

Along with having authority over the bureaucracy, politicians also control the work that bureaucrats do. They come into power with an agenda and a multitude of campaign promises. Bureaucrats are expected and required to deliver on them, which can tie the hands of employees for months on end, thereby controlling the work that gets done. Many promises made by electioneering politicians don't benefit from bureaucratic analysis before commitments are made. It's why we — and colleagues we worked with throughout the country — referred to them as ghastly, and why many parties back away from promises when they understand the reality of their foolhardy words.

3. Aiding and abetting

Political leaders also try to exercise power over the bureaucracy by placing political aides throughout the system. These include the people who are put into central agencies shortly after an election. They include those ever-present ministerial assistants in every department, many of whom adopt an air of authority, though in reality they have no real legislative authority over the bureaucracy. These positions are referred to as legislative assistants in some provinces, as well as parliamentary assistants federally.[4] We've been in departments where deputy ministers had to repeatedly put political staffers in their place. Still, bureaucrats soon learned that edicts from these political aides can sometimes trump sound departmental advice. More often than is healthy, this type of behaviour can create resentment between political appointees and bureaucrats. Of course, one of the great joys of being a bureaucrat is watching these overbearing political aides scurry out of offices with their personal belongings after a new party comes into power.

Back at You — Bureaucratic Controls That Keep Politicians in Check

Even with the various political controls we've just identified, bureaucrats still have power within the system, which is not something politicians at any level of government like to hear. This brings us to an exploration of the various controls bureaucrats use to keep politicians in check.

1. Control the means that lead to the end

For the most part, bureaucrats control the means that lead to the end. By this we mean that bureaucrats must adhere to many rules and fill out copious amounts of paperwork that politicians must sign to get things done. Smart lobbyists, advocates and citizens seeking action from governments recognize this and work to build relationships with the bureaucrats responsible for the paperwork involved in any government decision.

The paperwork is tedious, but this internal red tape supports a system of checks and balances. If bureaucrats are lucky enough to get their work ticked off from all those layers within the hierarchy, chances are a politician will sign off on a decision. Many bureaucrats grasp early on that they can control how an issue is framed and the speed with which the paperwork gets to a politician. Not only does this give bureaucrats a sense of control, but it also reinforces the important role they have within the system.

A so-called no-brainer issue that demonstrated the power bureaucrats have to slow things down involved a premier's decision to extend daylight savings time. The premier confirmed his decision by publicly stating being in sync with the United States and other Maritime provinces was a "no-brainer" and that the province would extend it. Even though the premier gave clear marching orders, the leaders above us insisted we took the time to reach out to every department and document the impacts, as well as present the pros and cons of various options, including not moving forward with the switch. This took weeks. Thereafter, we joked that no-brainer issues tended to require the most paperwork of all. Of course, the legislation was changed, and the clocks moved in sync with our neighbours to the south.

2. Control the issues that get in front of elected officials

Another area of control some bureaucrats relish involves serving as a gatekeeper. Many senior bureaucrats determine what departmental issues are brought to their ministers' attention, including how the information about those issues are presented.

These senior staffers have an established network with ties to interest groups, and they can use those interest groups to further their own agendas. As an example, many bureaucrats have relationships with people from the sectors they serve, including sympathizing and at times developing a passion for the issues or needs of the groups. They become advocates for those sectors and build their power base within the system by picking and choosing what to present to decision makers.

This makes it easy for interest groups to use bureaucrats to pursue their agendas. It's a collusion of sorts — often, it is characterized as an industry or interest group capturing the bureaucrats who are supposed to regulate them in the public interest.

This has become more pronounced over time because governments increasingly operate in a network of non-governmental organizations (NGOs) and citizen groups.

3. Have the expertise to manipulate

Ministers cannot possibly have the expertise required for the myriad of issues governments face. Much of that expertise resides within the bureaucracy, and those who have it can present information leading to the outcome they want — hopefully, that is in the public interest as public service principles require.

Given the short-term tenure of politicians (though there are exceptions), both politicians and the public rely on the corporate memories of bureaucrats to shed light on programs and policies and the information shared can be self-serving or self-preserving.

We've witnessed bureaucrats skillfully make the case for more resources by tapping into politicians' desires to create jobs; tap into their pride; or by addressing their fears. In some cases, this enabled bureaucrats to build their empire or secure needed funds for a pet project. You might think issues that pulled on the heart strings would also win favours, but social issues tended to take a back seat to economic and public safety issues during our time in government. This was the case provincially, as well as with our work at various federal, provincial and territorial tables. It's worth the effort for anyone looking for approval for a project, resources or a simple go-ahead to know what makes ministers sit up and take notice.

4. Are less influenced by public opinion

We'll wrap up this section on controls with the acknowledgement that bureaucrats are somewhat insulated from public opinion. This means they can be more critical of public views, which can be wishy-washy at best or prone to mob mentality at worst. The insulation from public opinion can vary depending on which level of government a bureaucrat serves. For example, those working at the municipal level would have more contact with citizens on a regular basis compared to a bureaucrat in a head office at the federal level.

The term "faceless bureaucrat" stems from the fact that bureaucrats are subservient to elected officials. In this case, it's a blessing to be hidden from the public. Ideally, bureaucrats can point out the downsides, costs and impacts of actions being demanded by public opinion.

Being an invisible bureaucrat is often appropriate, but no voice for bureaucrats leaves an imbalance in the dialogue around what government is, does and doesn't do.

Case in Point

This brings us to our first case in point, where we offer up an example that puts some of the content we shared in this chapter to the test. This case concerns ministerial accountability and the practice of throwing bureaucrats under the bus.

A former Nova Scotia Department of Justice lawyer, Alex Cameron, filed a law suit against the premier and former justice minister for defamation and constructive dismissal. Cameron filed the suit against government for implying he acted without instruction when he presented a brief suggesting the Mi'kmaq were a "conquered people" as part of government's defense in a court submission concerning the Sipekne'katik band's efforts to stop a proposed natural gas storage project. When the argument was made — namely that the province did not have a duty to consult with the band because they were a "conquered people" — there was public outcry. Cameron, who had a 30-year career with the province, was removed from the file and the brief withdrawn. He retired shortly after and filed the suit.

News outlets reported that in his affidavit, which was later released by the court, despite efforts by the province to suppress it, Cameron alleged the premier and senior members of the government knew of and supported the argument. However, when the story went public, he said his deputy minister told him his argument would likely be abandoned and that he would be thrown under the bus.[5] The province filed papers denying the allegations, arguing the case should be dismissed.[6]

Whether the allegations are true has not been determined at the time of writing. But we do know that when some elected officials are backed into corners, they can quickly toss ministerial accountability aside. Unfortunately, cases like this reinforce the belief in the public and in the media that elected officials are figureheads only and should not be held accountable for actions of the bureaucrats in government.

TALKING POINTS

As we noted in our introduction, we're saving this section in each chapter for some critical takeaways. For our belly of the beast discussion, they include:

- Bureaucrats are often wrongly lumped in with elected officials, which could partially explain why they are maligned.
- While members of the public are quick to criticize civil servants, they have likely relied on a bureaucrat and will continue to do so throughout their lives.
- Bureaucrats would be wise to heed these words shared by one of our bosses: they live in a democracy; they don't work in one.
- Bureaucrats should also seek to understand not only their place, but also where others fit within the hierarchy and they should look for opportunities to reach beyond the silos they are working in.
- It is critical to recognize the control politicians have, but that shouldn't stop bureaucrats from speaking truth to power, especially if partisan interest is jeopardizing public interest.
- Bureaucrats should also recognize the controls they have and learn to use them wisely.

Don't take our word for it

To back up some of the points we've made, we're going to rely on the insights of others for this section. We referenced impartiality as a key principle that bureaucrats everywhere are expected to uphold.

Renowned public administration professor and author Peter Aucoin pointed out that impartiality has two critical meanings, the first of which is that "citizens be treated impartially in the administration of public affairs, and second, public servants not act in ways that advantage or disadvantage the partisan-political interests of any political party, including the governing party or parties. The latter means that, at a minimum, public servants not be a party to:

- Political influence in the staffing of the public service as a function of partisan patronage or cronyism;
- Patronage or pork-barreling in the award and distribution of government projects, grants, contribution, and contracts;
- Politicization of the content of public-service communications to the media and the public, including government advertising; or
- Positive or negative comments on matters of government policy or behaviour to the media, legislative committees, or various attentive publics."[7]

Chapter 2

CULTURE CLUB: THE WORKPLACE CULTURE OF GOVERNMENT BUREAUCRACY

*"Government is not about morality, it is about stability;
keeping things going, preventing anarchy, stopping society
falling to bits. Still being here tomorrow!"*

— Sir Humphrey Appleby, *Yes Minister*

IN THIS CHAPTER:
- Structural Issues That Cast a Shadow over Workplace Culture
- Control Systems and Processes That Shape Culture
- How Change Affects Culture and Vice Versa
- Diversity within Government Culture or Lack Thereof

Throughout our years of service, we received plenty of digs when we told people what we did for a living. As one colleague puts it, "They'll talk about your cushy job, your lack of work ethic and your gold-plated pension. Brace yourself, and don't bother debating. This will not change. Prove them wrong instead."

The potshots don't only come from friends and the general public. While running for office, some politicians are especially quick to pounce because they can get brownie points for slamming the civil service. This takes its toll on how bureaucrats feel about the workplace *and* their work.

With all the negative perceptions of bureaucrats, it's reasonable to ask why anybody would want to sign on to civil service. A common reason is the notion of a job for life. There is nothing wrong with people wanting permanent, relatively secure jobs with good benefits, although civil service is not the stable career path it once was, given budget pressures and cuts in staffing.

Landing a permanent job with benefits was a motivating factor for us. A smaller group of civil servants we worked with wanted to change the world and thought they could by working in critical public portfolios, such as justice and environment. In some cases, government was — and still is — the main employer for a particular set of skills, including social services, curators and public health. And of course, there were the few who had political aspirations and thought joining the bureaucracy was a way to get their foot in the door of that world.

No matter what the motivation for joining government, bureaucrats need a thick skin to ward off criticisms that will come their way. They'll also need a sense of humour, which is particularly valuable when reviewing comments about the bureaucracy online. Here's a sampling:

- "1. Never use one word when a dozen will suffice.
  2. If it can be understood, it's not finished yet.
  3. Never be the first to do anything." — Smith's Principles of Bureaucratic Tinkertoys
- "The only thing that saves us from the bureaucracy is its inefficiency." — Eugene McCarthy
- "Bureaucracy is the art of making the possible impossible." — Javier Pascal Salcedo
- "To beat the bureaucracy, make your problem their problem." — Smith's Principles of Bureaucratic Tinkertoys
- "If you are going to sin, sin against God, not the bureaucracy, as God will forgive you, the bureaucracy will not." — Hyman Rickover
- "A bureaucrat is a person who cuts red tape sideways." — J. McCabe
- "Any sufficiently advanced bureaucracy is indistinguishable from molasses." — Anonymous

- "Government proposes, bureaucracy disposes. And the bureaucracy must dispose of government proposals by dumping them on us." — P. J. O'Rourke
- "Government programs, once launched, never disappear. Actually, a government bureau is the nearest thing to eternal life we'll ever see on this earth." — Ronald Reagan
- "The effort expended by the bureaucracy in defending any error is in direct proportion to the size of the error." — John Nies
- "To get the attention of a large animal, be it an elephant or a bureaucracy, it helps to know what part of it feels pain. Be very sure, though, that you want its full attention." — Kelvin Throop, a.k.a. R.A.J. Philips

Ouch!

We're not going to try to combat the negative perceptions people have about the government workplace. Instead, we will affirm that workplace culture — whether government or otherwise — is an outcome of many interplaying factors. It is also continually evolving — or devolving, as the cynics may claim.

As is the case in any organization, workplace culture influences the environment, the way employees relate to one another, and how they carry out the activities of the operation. In this chapter, we'll explore several substantial influencers that cast a long shadow over a bureaucrat's workplace, including those that have emerged from the very structure of government. We'll also share our thoughts on ways that governments try to shape culture through various control systems and processes, all of which affect bureaucratic leadership and management styles. We'll conclude the chapter with a look at two umbrella issues that have an impact on organizational culture, including how governments respond to change and how they accommodate diversity within the ranks.

We're dedicating a chapter to workplace culture because it influences how bureaucrats go about their work and how they interact with the public and their colleagues day in and day out. Being aware of the factors that influence culture may help those who interact with the bureaucracy better understand why civil servants behave the way they do. It may even help bureaucrats navigate or address those issues that can sometimes threaten the healthy environment many people strive to obtain.

Structural Issues That Cast a Shadow over Workplace Culture

We noted in Chapter 1 that government structure is composed of silos and hierarchies. These structures cast a long shadow over government organizations and directly influence the culture, including how players within the system interact with one another.

Silo mentality

You may have heard the term "silo mentality," which is a catch-all phrase to describe the ethos of the government workplace, including the perception that bureaucrats don't always play nice with one another. While bureaucrats may be part of a larger federal, provincial or local government organization, silos have created dozens of micro cultures within these organizations. Those micro cultures are each ruled by different theoretical, ideological and professional interests. These interests can sometimes collide or contradict one another, and bureaucrats have been known to go through great effort to defend their silos' turf and limit financial obligations.

Working across these various ideological and professional boundaries takes time and effort, which partially explains why the silo mentality is linked with inefficiency. As an example, when working with provincial colleagues from across the system on domestic violence, it took months for team members to understand the various theoretical frameworks at play to work together on a comprehensive government response. Justice staff saw the issue from a criminal justice lens, which is a relatively black-and-white view of victims and perpetrators. Staff in community services were focused on identifying necessary individual and community supports to address the harms, while colleagues in health looked at the issue from a determinants of health approach and rightly noted that in some cases perpetrators are also victims. Colleagues with the Advisory Council on the Status of Women saw it as a women's issue. Each of the perspectives was valid and required each participant stepping outside their silos to work collectively to identify where resources could have the most impact.

Throughout that process and in many other situations involving work across provincial government departments or other levels of government, bureaucrats tended to keep their cards close to their chest when issues came to the forefront. This is in part due to financial implications; there is incentive to wait to see whether others will step up to the plate and take on the financial responsibility.

It's also not easy for bureaucrats to share information with each other, let alone with stakeholders and the general public. This is, in part, the result of that other looming structural component, namely hierarchy, which often demands that any information bureaucrats share is scrutinized and approved by multiple layers within the organization. Because many of the leaders we interacted with were especially sensitive and risk-adverse, a standard operating principle was that the less information shared, the better, including sharing information with colleagues in other departments and levels of government.

Chain of command

We discussed hierarchies in Chapter 1, where we noted there are many layers to the government hierarchy and bureaucrats have to manoeuvre through them to get their work approved. This has a negative impact on workplace culture, as it slows things down considerably.

For the most part, we and our colleagues in Nova Scotia got approval to act through routing slips, which are colour-coded sheets of paper outlining details on the subject of whatever material is attached. These proposals to take action, together with their routing slips, made their way through various levels in the hierarchy, all of whom had to sign off, before reaching the minister, who also had to sign off. Only then did this routing slip get sent back to the originator, so that they could act on whatever permission had been sought.

Routing slips were required for all correspondence headed up the chain of command — be that briefing notes seeking direction on various issues, proposed presentations to be delivered, draft responses to letters for a minister or premier; the list goes on. Managers took these routing slips very seriously, so bureaucrats had to fill them out properly or they would make their way back for revision even if the attachment had been perfectly crafted. Consider the case where one of us neglected to note in the "details" section of the briefing note routing slip that a briefing note was attached. Even though our superiors could see the attached document, they wanted us to tell them it was there. A new version was printed and rerouted to state the obvious, delaying the process by several days.

Theory suggests that if organizations want to boost productivity, they should keep major decisions to three or fewer people. We're here to tell you that is unlikely to happen because of the many layers of positional power within government bureaucracies. Government organizations are top-management heavy. We witnessed a continuing increase in the number of senior bureaucrats placed between the lower ranks and the ministers we served. While serving as a senior policy analyst, one of us had six layers of management to get through before the results of our analyses and advice were brought to the attention of the minister.

We appreciate that the levels of approval in government hierarchies can ensure appropriate due diligence is applied on initiatives with far-reaching impacts. But more often than not, the chain of command hampers the ability of a bureaucracy to get things done. This left bureaucrats feeling frustrated and powerless to bring ideas forward, even though they were often more informed and better educated than their bosses regarding the issues they were hired to address.

One of us did jump over the layers once to push through a project — but there was fallout. Initially, the fallout consisted of little interest or regard for the work being carried out by immediate supervisors. Eventually, we were removed from the project, and efforts to expand the program also fell flat because no one had responsibility for carrying the work forward. In fairness, we knew there would be a price to pay, but we ignored the chain of command because we believed in what we were proposing and assumed the minister would, too.

The proposal was to start a puppy socialization program at a provincial correctional facility in partnership with the SPCA. A few of us worked on a research proposal and then submitted a routing slip, a briefing note and the proposal seeking permission to approach the SPCA with the idea and to gauge whether they would be willing to participate. In follow-up inquiries on the status of our request, we were informed the briefing note had not made it past the next layers in the chain of command, let alone reaching the minister. Eventually, we happened to be at a meeting with the minister. During a discussion on programming possibilities, we introduced our idea and slid our proposal, which we had at the ready, across the boardroom table. We received permission to engage with the SPCA on the spot, and the program eventually came into being. Called Working on our Future (WOOF), the program brought puppies into the Central Nova Scotia Correctional Facility, and those puppies were paired with screened inmates. Under the direction of an expert SPCA trainer, inmates helped the puppies learn skills that assisted with their eventual adoption. The inmates engaged in productive activity and in the process learned responsibility, patience and respect — skills that could help them once released. The program withstood many more hurdles, including attacks by opposition, who claimed government was giving puppies to prisoners. It survived changes in government and received a reward for innovation at a 2013 international Summit for Urban Animal Strategies held in Alberta. The people who initially stalled on moving the request forward did eventually apologize for not initially recognizing the merit of the initiative.

It takes guts to push back again the chain of command. Careers can suffer; as such, we don't recommend it as regular practice. Still, we have often lamented the loss of risk-takers over the years, some of whom were labelled as subversives for ignoring the chain of command. Ironically, management experts promote the need for disrupters if organizations are to innovate — and governments love to latch onto innovation schemes. But we pity the soul who challenges the status quo in a government bureaucracy.

Rural-urban divide

Another structural issue worthy of note because of its influence on culture is the location of government offices. Our experience notes that regional offices have a more casual and personal feel to them. We attribute this to the distances these offices have from senior management and politicians who are most often located in urban head offices. We expect everyone can appreciate that the absence of those in the highest positions breathing down your neck can lighten the atmosphere. The work undertaken in regional offices also tends to be more operational in nature, and employees see the results of their work more readily. Going home at the end of the day witnessing your accomplishments is a rewarding feeling that few in government head offices experience. The silo mentality is not as pronounced because some departments are co-located, where collegiality is stronger given the relationships that exist. In addition, employees may not have the same stresses found in big cities, such as commute times and parking challenges. These are just some of the factors a number of colleagues identified as reasons why they would prefer not to move into a head office location.

The more personal atmosphere may stem from having closer connections to clients given smaller population bases in regional locations. We should note, however, that centralization efforts within government structures cut into regional office autonomy, as well as personal interactions with clients. Consider the case where people in our neighbourhood were once able to call the transportation depot directly to report unsafe road conditions. Now all those calls are routed through a central service. Getting someone to call back can be an exercise in patience and, of course, the people processing the calls may not be familiar with the area of concern.

Union-management dichotomy

We're going to switch tracks now and explore another dominant structural feature that shapes the culture of a government workplace: the union-management dichotomy. This can be a game changer in any organization where unions exist. We believe unions provide value and often play a necessary role in organizations, where their interventions can bring many ugly situations, including employee-management conflicts and harassment, to a good end.

However, in addition to the very real tensions between elected officials and bureaucrats, government environments can be a breeding ground for tensions between management and unions, and in some cases, elected officials escalate the trouble.

As an example of politicians provoking unions, consider this tiff led by former Nova Scotia Finance Minister Randy Delorey. Prior to beginning a new round of collective bargaining, he issued a statement to NS government employees pointing out that previous labour agreements outpaced economic growth and added hundreds of millions of dollars to the province's expenses. He said government would not be asking taxpayers to shoulder a heavier tax burden to fund wage increases, noting that, "If frontline employees can find ways to operate more efficiently and if those changes create concrete savings, we are willing to share those savings with our hard-working employees."[1]

The minister's message did not sit well with many, including reporter Tim Bousquet of the *Halifax Examiner*. Bousquet wrote: "And who will find those cost reductions, cost avoidances, service redesigns and efficiencies? The unions. This is an utter abandonment of managerial responsibility — the Liberals are throwing up their hands and saying, 'f**k it, we don't know how to save money, it's up to you guys.' Moreover, it's a bald attempt to destroy union solidarity, to pit public employees against one another. Workers over in Department A can get raises, but only if they figure out a way to get workers over in Department B fired."[2]

Many government employees throughout Canada have lived in various states of budget restraint, and cuts often translate into lost programming or jobs. While they may have ideas on how to fix some things, suggesting that employees can address structural deficits is disingenuous. Politicians know the big-ticket financial challenges are far beyond what a bureaucrat can control, and these decisions have to be political ones. Yes, employees, particularly those in the union, can provide advice, but they don't have the authority to dictate overall budgets.

Unfortunately, negative stereotypes and perceptions about cushy jobs, generous benefits and pensions have led many Canadians to applaud when civil servants face cutbacks and wage freezes. Elected politicians know this and sadly often use it to the disadvantage of union members. Unlike the private sector, every salary negotiation becomes public knowledge and is open to criticism. This allows governments to limit or avoid increases and limit rewards and incentives because they know there is little public support for increased benefits of any kind for civil servants. The federal government has recently bucked this trend, but that hasn't stopped the attacks. Consider this comment from Aaron Wudrick, Director of the Canadian Taxpayers Federation, regarding the federal government's July 2020 decision to increase wages for civil servants: "The idea that government employees should be getting a pay raise right now is incredibly tone deaf."[3]

Attacks can backfire because public sector union employees are able to garner support from those who rely on services that government cannot easily relocate or shut down. However, we believe public sympathy across Canada has been waning for years.

One thing is certain: labour unions still have a significant impact on government work environments, formalizing the relationship between management and the rank and file. They affect the way formal human resource functions are carried out, and when issues do arise, everyone looks to collective agreements to justify their position.

Despite well-publicized battles between governments and unions, in our experience, the day-to-day working relationships between most managers and union members are healthy. However, problems can arise when management has standards that are unreasonable, or the union creates unrealistic expectations among its members.

Union actions often result in positive outcomes for employees, but there are exceptions. Consider an example where a union employee accused of theft was actually rewarded for it. The employee was caught stealing from the government red-handed, and to make things worse, it was the second time he was caught. The first time, he was fired. The union grieved, and due to some political interference, he was reinstated with the understanding, in writing, that if this happened again, he would be fired on the spot, and the union wouldn't grieve the action again.

The second time around, he was fired, but the union went back on their word and grieved the termination. After much deliberation, management felt the only way to keep the termination in place was to offer a settlement to the employee, which included a legal agreement that he would never apply for any government positions.

The employees in the division where the theft took place knew about this situation and many were disappointed and confused with the outcome. They saw someone being rewarded for bad behaviour. Many lost respect for the union and resented having to be associated with these activities.

In our experience, most union members have no direct contact with union representatives and they simply pay their membership dues each month as required. Like insurance, it's there if needed in a crisis.

Finally, it's important to keep in mind that union brass are third parties representing various groups within bureaucracies that bargain for collective agreements. Common elements found in these agreements include seniority provisions; provisions dealing with work scheduling, vacation and leave; compensation, including classification; and a grievance and complaints process. Elected politicians sometimes ignore these provisions, especially in the area of recruitment, wherein those with political affiliation have been selected for jobs, including ones that weren't advertised. This leads to cynicism within the ranks.

Control Systems and Processes That Shape Culture

Now we've reached our exploration of control systems and processes that shape government culture. The first of those are recruitment and promotion processes. It is worth noting here that federal and provincial governments have dedicated independent agencies responsible for overseeing the public service, including hiring, training and development.

Recruitment and promotion practices

Political hires are a concern on the staffing front because nothing can erode a culture faster than a sense of unfairness. This happens when political hires are placed in civil service roles. Such a practice flies in the face of control systems in place to prevent this very thing from happening in recruitment and promotion, including fair hiring policies. In Nova Scotia, this policy requires that hiring managers recruit in a manner that is "fair, objective, consistent, equitable, non-discriminatory and legally defensible." All provinces in Canada have similar policies, principles or philosophies that require recruitment be merit based. In addition to merit, Nunavut has articulated principles that give priority to Inuit people and promote Inuit culture.

Fortunately, the placement of political operatives in civil servant positions does not happen as much as some bureaucrats and the public presume. It only takes one political hire to start the resentment, particularly if, as is sometimes the case, the individual being placed is not qualified for the role. We have both been in positions where we were told someone is starting a role the following week and to get a job description, contract and communication ready in advance. People coming into these roles were almost always connected to the party in power. Some were unsuccessful in their attempt to get into politics or into the public sector using the normal channels. To be frank, some could not contribute much value, which led to even more resentment by department employees aware of how the person got the job.

A particularly egregious example that garnered press at the time involved the hiring of a former newspaper columnist for a $106,000 permanent senior position in NS's executive council office. Through a freedom of information request, the union obtained information showing the person who got hired — Marilla Stephenson — was consulted on the job description for a position before it was posted internally. Other documents captured details of internal discussions regarding an appropriate employee classification for Stephenson, who was doing some contract work for the office at the time. The position was open only to people in that office, and her contract was extended, thus conveniently qualifying her to apply. Apparently, she was the only applicant.[4]

In response to inquiries about the situation, a government spokeswoman for the commission responsible for fair hiring policies said proper procedures were followed. The former leader of the opposition at the time had a different take, suggesting the position was gifted to a person with connections to the premier.[5] There wasn't one bureaucrat we spoke with at the time who believed the process was fair.

Another case in NS took place in 2013; it generated accusations of patronage involving the placement of a former liberal candidate and caucus staffer, Glennie Langille, as the Chief of Protocol. At the time, the position was outside the civil service, with the premier claiming he was doing what his predecessors had done by placing her in the position. Because it was not a permanent civil service job, she would serve at the whim of the governing party.[6] Eventually, the position was brought into the civil service, and Langille had to compete for the job. Allegedly those interested had six days to apply. Of course, she got the position with an advertised salary range of $91,800 to $114,700 and protection for her job, even with a change of government.[7]

We could never figure out if politicians assumed civil servants were stupid and failed to see what was happening, or if they were just arrogant and didn't care what bureaucrats thought. Many of these political hires often come with their own sense of entitlement, which only adds to resentment among employees.

Politicians have every right to hire staff into political positions. They can do so by working outside of bureaucratic fair hiring policies. But when they slide "their people" into civil service roles, they are breaking the rules and practicing patronage and political nepotism — and that, of course, is wrong.

One last observation on political hires — most do leave when the government in power is voted out, or a minister is transferred to another department. Bureaucrats should not look to this as the hill to die on. Besides, we worked with a select few who stuck around and made positive contributions. Like most civil servants, they were grateful for the job and wanted to serve the public good.

But there are bigger bureaucratic staffing issues that leave an imprint on workplace culture. One is the practice of rewarding and recognizing competent specialists by promoting them into management and leadership positions, though they may not have the necessary skills and competencies for managerial roles. We understand that leaders want to reward employees who are strong individual contributors, but promoting them into management can backfire. Not everyone is, or should be, a leader or manager. We had many bosses who were extremely good at their functional job but lacked the soft skills and leadership qualities needed once they hit the management cadre. Yes, these individuals can often acquire required competencies through development, but that poses challenges for everyone while these skills are being developed. The Peter Principle — or the phenomenon of promoting people past their level of competence — is alive and well within government.

In government hierarchies, moving people up the chain of command is one of the only ways to reward good employees. We saw instances where those placed in such roles became problem employees, as they lacked the competencies and, in the process, actually damaged the teams they were supposed to be leading. We had our share of senior managers who turned into tyrants as they got more power. We recall an occasion wherein a newly minted boss demanded that all employees provide access to their calendars, so he could track their comings and goings. He would have been highly critical of this action prior to becoming a senior leader.

Other recruitment issues that affect workplace culture are worthy of mention, including the perception that people get hired into government because of who they know and not for what they bring to the position. This sometimes was the case years ago. Sadly, the perception of "sketchy" recruitment practices lingers. As a result, new civil servants are often viewed with cynicism. Another perception is that only those in unions will get a chance at advertised positions. This makes recruitment a challenge, particularly for managers who are looking to bring new people into the organization. It's also fair to say that government recruitment processes — put in place to protect against political interference and nepotism by both bureaucrats and politicians — are rigid and cumbersome. Because of this, some will try to find ways around them and that can backfire with accusations of favouritism and breaking the rules.

We'll conclude with some thoughts on leadership recruitment. We knew politicians who had different perceptions than bureaucrats regarding what makes a good leader, with a strong desire for people who would simply say yes to all their demands. We also noticed a developing trend among senior leaders within the bureaucracy who simply wanted cheerleaders and viewed anything other than blind acceptance as obstructionist behaviour. And then there are the "out-siders" who are plopped into senior leadership roles, despite having never worked in government. We worked with a few who believed they could shift the culture on a dime. It was our experience that many came into the service with a disdain for the system and the people, which only contributed to a culture of disrespect. This did not serve them well in the long term. We recall a leader coming from the private sector who, upon his arrival, commented that most civil servants were nothing but deadwood, and claimed he was looking to terminate them so he could bring his own friends into the fold. This had an immediate and negative impact on the employees.

We encourage anybody who finds themselves in a leadership role to seek out ways to build their management capacity. We know first-hand there are opportunities to participate in professional development within the public service, including leadership training. Federally, there is a Canada School of Public Service accessible to those interested.[8]

Training and development opportunities

This brings us to another control process that governments use to shape culture: management training and development opportunities, an area where governments make heavy investments. Civil servants are required to participate in courses on a wide range of topics, including diversity and cultural competency, sexual harassment, and occupational health and safety.

We occasionally ran into difficulties using the knowledge we gained in training courses in practical ways. A lot of the materials were developed with the private sector in mind, and therefore difficult to apply in the public sector environment. We discuss why that is in Chapter 4, including identifying the many challenges associated with applying business practices in government settings.

A final observation on training and development to note: we recognize that the position a bureaucrat held, the geographic area where they worked and their relationship with their supervisor all influenced the opportunities that came their way. There was not a fair distribution of opportunity across the board, particularly because most training is held in head office locations in major cities. The costs associated with travel and accommodation put employees in rural areas at a disadvantage.

Values and codes of conduct

While training and development opportunities may not be readily available to all employees, anybody who works in the civil service is expected to abide by public service values and codes of conduct, which serve as another way that governments attempt to influence culture. Agencies responsible for the civil service push these platitudes out to all employees with the expectation that employees will accept and demonstrate the precepts in their daily work. We believe values can help to shape the culture that leaders want and expect, especially if the statements resonate with employees. They can easily help identify what behaviours are expected and set the context for the work that gets done.

Former Deputy Minister Rosalind Penfound, who also served as head of Nova Scotia's Public Service Commission, shared the following with us:

> A cynic might scoff at a bureaucracy having values like respect, integrity, diversity, accountability and the public good (the articulated values of the Nova Scotia Public Service). Not me. Because to me these values speak far less about elected government than they do about public servants; how they strive to serve the public, do good work, and how they treat and feel about each other.

For her, any discussion of values and public service starts with democracy:

> When I think of public service, bureaucracy and values, democracy is at the top of my list of values. More than a few times, particularly when serving as a senior public servant and having become frustrated or concerned about something, I had to remind myself of that. I would hasten to add that it took me awhile to be able to do that.
>
> When we were younger, I would hazard to guess, we all had bouts of righteous indignation or complete certainty that some or other decision maker was an idiot or worse, and perhaps they were. But as I became long in the tooth and the grey hair began taking over, I became less certain about some of my opinions, and more likely to allow that there might be vantage points I did not have or considerations at play that I might not fully appreciate or understand. Such was the case more than a few times about decisions made by elected government. But, there were a few things that I thought at the time, and still think, were just plain stupid, wrongheaded or, at the least, ill-advised.

In addition to upholding values associated with serving the public good, civil servants are also expected to abide by codes of conduct. Official codes of conduct require that bureaucrats not place government action in disrepute and that extends beyond the workplace to interactions outside of work hours.

Official codes of conduct are relatively new for civil servants, and one of us is thankful they weren't official years ago. While working for government, we publicly called into question government actions in a fight to save a community beach. A landowner had tried to block access, and when we stood up to him, he orchestrated a charge under a provincial *Protection of Property Act*. The case was thrown out on a technicality, but it generated some press, including criticisms we made against the

Crown for pursuing the charge in the first place, as well as against the Department of Natural Resources for their failure to step in and protect the community beach. After the case was thrown out of court, the landowner lodged a complaint against us, suggesting we had taken advantage of insider knowledge. Had that been the case, we wouldn't have ended up in court in the first place. Like the charge, the complaint was thrown out, and the beach was eventually saved when the municipality stepped in. If a code of conduct had been in place, we would have likely been reprimanded for tarnishing the reputation of a government agency.

Given the number of people who work for various levels of government, we often wondered if the chilling effect of a code of conduct hampers legitimate criticisms from bureaucrats acting as citizens. These are the people who work in the system and know it well.

Conflict of interest guidelines are also important because they complement codes of conduct. Bureaucrats should become familiar with these, particularly if they are volunteering with an organization that has an issue with, or is looking for something from, government, especially if the organization's interest is with the department where they serve.

One can argue stated values, codes of conduct and conflict of interest guidelines are useful guideposts, but without complementary systems and management styles, such words are vacuous. When people who preach the values fail to demonstrate them in their day-to-day interactions, they leave cynicism and disillusionment in their wake.

We worked with individuals who didn't hesitate to say "Do as I say, not as I do" and were bullies as leaders. In fact, those attitudes have been exhibited by whole service groups. For example, while working in human resources, we were sometimes accused of having double standards. There was some truth to that, including attempts to get around the very policies we insisted people adhere to, including fair hiring.

During our years of service, we did not often look for role models in the political leadership cadre. Though we worked with many politicians with great intentions, sadly, we all knew some who stretched the truth, misled, made promises they couldn't keep and manipulated communication to their advantage. The reasons why are understandable for the most part.

When running for leadership, politicians often do not have a depth of knowledge about the constraints they'll face once in power, or they must satisfy competing pressures from constituents and the party faithful if they want to keep their job.

We understand that government is a political structure, and the dance between political and partisan interests is ongoing. Yet we believe many people don't understand the difference between partisan interests and political considerations.

This played out for us when we watched news coverage of the SNC Lavalin political scandal that erupted in February 2019, concerning allegations of political interference with the justice system by Prime Minister Trudeau and his office. The gist of the scandal involved efforts by some to secure a deferred prosecution agreement for bribery charges levelled against the company to save jobs. There was a great deal of fallout, including the resignation of the minister who raised the alarm; the resignation of the principal secretary to Trudeau; and the early retirement of the clerk of the Privy Council, who served as Canada's top bureaucrat. During hearings into the affair, the former principal secretary and the former clerk of the privy council said they tried to find a "political solution."[9]

The indignation of the opposition made for great television, as did commentary from the public awash in shock that government could do such a thing. To which we say: of course there would be political interference given the economic issues at stake! To think otherwise is naive. Looking at issues from a political lens is a reality within government, as is mitigating political fallout.

We're not suggesting that rules weren't broken. Ethics popped up repeatedly during that fiasco, as it often does in government scandals, with the prime minister's office accused of skirting the truth. But on the bureaucratic side of the house, the federal ethics commissioner determined that no ethical rules were broken by Canada's former top civil servant.

We expect the truth will remain elusive. That is undoubtedly a concern. As James Comey writes in *A Higher Loyalty: Truth, Lies, and Leadership*: "Without a fundamental commitment to the truth —

especially in our public institutions and those who lead them — we are lost. As a legal principle, if people don't tell the truth, our justice system cannot function, and a society based on the rule of law begins to dissolve. As a leadership principle, if leaders don't tell the truth, or won't hear the truth from others, they cannot make good decisions, they cannot themselves improve, and they cannot inspire trust among those who follow them."[10]

Elected officials and leaders within all levels of the bureaucracy would be wise to heed Comey's words because employees look to them to walk the talk and demonstrate ethics and decency in their actions.

Ongoing threat of budget cuts

One area where politicians may wish to be wiser with their words has to do with budget cuts, which brings us to another control process that influences the government workplace. We have a lot more to say about budgets in Chapter 7, but we do want to make the point that budgets can impact workplace culture. Living under constant threat of the axe falling takes its toll on the people whose jobs are at stake. We've heard individuals, especially those running for power, casually discuss program cuts and finding efficiencies, seemingly without considering the impact on people who support these programs. Politicians also repeatedly make demands to fix systems within the bureaucracy, but the demands are often not accompanied by budgets or employees needed to carry out the work.

The perception of waste in government is also widespread. As Gregory Keefe, a former Deputy Minister of Nova Scotia's provincial treasury, said: "It has become so ingrained as to no longer be subject to question. Indeed, like any large organization, it is true to some extent. The challenge is that it is not as large as is perceived, nor can it be quickly harvested. This belief persists because it is an easy explanation for the question 'Where is the money coming from?' I have seen this in numerous campaigns where proponents say they will pay for their programs by reducing waste." Keefe claims it also plays well, as citizens can say, "I can vote to eliminate waste because I won't lose any program benefits that way." He adds that, "Waste is in the eye of the beholder. One of the great strengths of our society is its diversity. With diversity comes disagreement on what is useful spending. A child development advocate might support funding for organized childhood activities like sports or camps, while another might argue this is wasteful as unorganized play is more valuable."

While we were in the civil service, every new budget cycle generated fear for some bureaucrats who felt their jobs were at stake. Others felt undervalued and under-appreciated because the work they were doing for years was being criticized, often unfairly, as a justification to cut expenses.

We noticed that politicians were very sensitive and hesitant to make any cuts in rural areas. Fear tended to be more pronounced in head office environments, where most of the cuts were made. When people are scared, they resort to behaviours that do not serve the culture, including fear of risk, increased sick time, sabotaging colleagues and working hard to win the appraisal of those who they feel can protect them. We witnessed workplaces with healthy cultures quickly morph into unhealthy, poisonous environments due to fear of impending cuts or change.

When budgets are tight, staff and team development takes a hit, too. Contrary to popular belief, bureaucrats work hard and often don't have time to socialize or engage with their colleagues. Team-building exercises are a way to make this happen, but they were often the first item on the chopping block. Employee development is even more important, but resources slated for such work also hit the cutting room floor in challenging financial times. This resulted in an erosion of the skills and knowledge bureaucrats needed to work for the public. The public wants those doing inspections to be aware of new technologies and new tools to investigate unsafe or unsanitary environments, but that can't happen without training.

During our time in government, the small perks that once existed — such as the occasional free coffee or holiday party — also disappeared. We think this was appropriate given the financial challenges of governments, but it did have consequences. Employees who had enjoyed those small perks lost what they had. As bureaucrats were told to tighten their belts, a double standard remained: politicians continued to enjoy their perks, understandably leading to resentment and cynicism.

How Change Affects Culture and Vice Versa

Of course, every round of budget cuts results in significant change within organizations. Along with shifts in priorities that budgets demand, bureaucrats regularly have to adapt to redesigned systems and policies, new leadership and projects and colleagues who have been let go, alongside the arrival of new hires.

The frequency of change and how it's managed is an umbrella issue that affects the culture of the organization as a whole. On the flip side, bureaucratic culture also affects the rate and success of change efforts.

For the most part, governments are terrible at managing change, even though they spend huge amounts of money training bureaucrats to lead the process. During our time, Prosci was the flavour of the day, and like most off-the-shelf training, the material was not developed with public sector management in mind and was not particularly useful.

Despite all the training, we often felt that senior management decisions associated with change were made without a full appreciation of the impact on work and workers. Many leaders became secretive, non-communicative and detached, and when the changes eventually did hit the fan, there was little support or empathy demonstrated. This contributed to employee resistance and developed a culture around fear of change.

It was rare for managers to acknowledge that change often represented a loss to many people. With loss, there is often grief. In grief, there are five recognized stages: shock, denial, guilt, anger and acceptance. Few leaders grasp that the stages are not linear; employees move through them at different rates. Blanket approaches to deal with individuals coping with change don't quite cut it.

Change may be good and necessary, but it can hurt. As employees, we never felt free enough to admit this for fear of being labelled an obstructionist or a so-called "negative nellie." We witnessed attempts by leaders who pretended everything was fine. They needed to toe the line, but they could have acknowledged loss and encouraged people to talk about the good outcomes and aspects of change that were possible. Positivity has a direct correlation to how well people adjust to change, and trust us when we say that positive bureaucrats make for better public services.

We would be remiss if we did not specifically acknowledge that changes resulting from election periods are especially disconcerting for bureaucrats because, as we noted earlier, many politicians run on the premise of cuts and fixing bureaucracy. Leading up to elections, budgets were frozen, hiring was put on hold, and bureaucrats were expected to remain quiet and avoid creating controversies. This resulted in frustrating and tense periods, which were then followed by a flurry of activity to prepare for a new government, even if the same crew returned to office.

Some employees in head offices were consumed with following party platforms and preparing to fulfill particular promises in their area of responsibility. Colour-coded binders made it easy to pick the winning platform based on party colours. Besides platform tracking, bureaucrats also scrambled to put together "transition binders" that included key staff contacts; current challenges; legislative responsibilities; budget; who the minister needed to contact immediately, in the next week and the next month; key decisions to be made immediately upon entry to the office; and a list of all the issues that would likely haunt the minister's mandate.

During our time, prepping for a new government's arrival was like getting ready to welcome royalty. Senior leaders tended to be on their best behaviour and dressed for the part of the consummate professional. Briefing books were prepared and meetings scheduled. Within a few weeks, the new minister did a walkabout, and shortly after, new marching orders transferred down the line. In some situations, bureaucrats were told to shelve work on an issue that a new government hadn't identified as a priority. Despite thinking it wasn't a priority, the big issues never did go away. This happened time and time again. It contributed to complacency, especially for employees who were potentially over-invested in the issue. In many organizations, passion is a good thing. But bureaucrats are not hired for their passion; it can create conflict and frustration if the leadership decides what a bureaucrat is passionate about no longer has merit or sees it as a priority.

Many of the managers we dealt with were not well-schooled in ways to empathetically deal with people who worked tirelessly on an issue that spoke to their heart, but that was no longer a priority. Thoughtfully helping people disengage from projects so they could apply their expertise elsewhere could have gone a long way towards addressing complacency.

We've shared some ways that change inflicted on the civil service affects culture, but the very structure of government also affects the ability of bureaucracy to introduce necessary change. Hierarchy and specialization are all about stabilization. This can be a positive aspect, as people rely on the services governments provide, and laws cannot and should not change on a whim. But this can be a double-edged sword for bureaucrats. Like citizens, they benefit from certainty and stability, but bureaucrats also have to deal with frustration when they know change is needed, even if it will be a long time coming. Unlike the private sector, which is more apt to respond to change if it wants to survive in a competitive marketplace, the public sector, as a monopoly service provider, does not face the same pressures.

Professors Patricia W. Ingraham and Nadia Rubaii-Barrett nailed this conundrum in an article for the academic journal *Foundations of Public Administration*. They write:

> The stability and the insularity that such structures provide
> can serve public organizations well if they protect public
> employees from inappropriate political intrusion and pres-
> sure. They can also guarantee citizens some predictability
> in the programs and organizations that serve them. Bureau-
> cratic structures do not serve government well, however,
> when they resist pressure for necessary change, when they
> become insulated from the citizens they serve, and when
> they become more characterized by stability than by energy,
> expertise, and responsiveness to changing circumstances.[11]

Governments make bold claims associated with change, and they try to encourage bureaucrats to step outside their comfort zone. We worked through several attempts, including experimental techniques such as "change labs" wherein leaders picked who they thought were the best and brightest, who then huddled to plot out how to fix entrenched social problems. Some viewed these exercises as pie-in-the-sky wishful thinking that rarely translated into concrete actions, and many were criticized for not inviting those with practical hands-on experience to participate. Good ideas may come from such exercises, but more often than not, elected leaders are not prepared to venture far beyond the status quo, as that is what got them elected in the first place.

Despite the glib talk, transformational change is highly unlikely in government unless there is a crisis. COVID-19 may well be the catalyst that will spark unprecedented change in public services. But for the most part, government change happens slowly and incrementally, and from our experience, changes made from the ground up are often more realistic and thus sustainable.

Diversity within Government Culture or Lack Thereof

The notion of incremental change is especially evident when it comes to diversity within the civil service, which is another issue affecting the culture of government. Diversity is what makes us distinct from each other; this includes, but is not limited to, age, language, culture, race, ethnicity, sexual orientation, gender, abilities and religious or spiritual beliefs. It is worth noting that policies may affect women, men and gender minorities differently, and unlike the other characteristics identified above, gender intersects with all categories.

Women have made significant progress securing positions within government, including leadership roles, although there are still gaps in positions traditionally held by men. These include engineering and geologist positions, supervisory roles in transportation, forestry technicians and those working in the areas of compliance, among others. However, the makeup of the civil service remains fairly homogeneous, with many groups still underrepresented. This is a critical issue; we need and should want public servants who reflect the diversity of the communities they serve.

Without diverse voices at the table, services will continue to fall short in terms of meeting different needs of population groups. Consider health care alone, where a former colleague and diversity champion Sharon Davis-Murdoch notes health services were not serving everyone effectively and shared the following observations with us: "The system was there, nobody was turned away, but unless people were receiving culturally specific and competent care, they were not being cared for to the level, or in the way that was going to support their health improvements."

She posed many questions worthy of examination and deserving of answers, including:

> How was the system going to respond to immigrants who didn't speak English, or Muslims, who did not want to be examined by physicians of the opposite sex? Where were the cultural and language interpreters? If they were a person of colour, what were we doing about the overt, systemic and internalized racism that they experienced and that had an impact on all Nova Scotians? What about the homophobia and transphobia and the predominance of heterosexism in the system despite inclusive policy language? How is Indigenous identity and history of colonization addressed in care and service? Who do you see as clinicians and senior administrators in health care? Who goes for preventative health screening, and who is seldom seen? How do decision-makers know what the health needs of people are if the MSI [Medical Insurance System] wasn't capturing health data by race, ethnicity and language?
>
> The case for change has been, and is being made over and over and over again. Post retirement, and working in community, I am still making it. Having to make these arguments is exhausting, but I did it and do it because

I know that as Ruth Ginsburg said, 'Real change comes about one step at a time.' I knew it couldn't be done over-night, and I knew that the only thing that I could do to ensure that the things didn't go off the rails, and I didn't either blow-up and lose my cool or forget the big picture and get involved in some counter-productive argument with somebody, was to keep the vision on the big picture and keep pushing forward.

Contextually, I did understand that I lived in Canada and was encouraged by the Canadian value system. I recognized that even if some senior leaders weren't that excited about the work of diversity and inclusion, they had to at least appear that they would be supportive of it. I un-derstood the political system, and I understood that while they may not have been authentic in their support, they also had incentive to pay attention to the work.

We did witness improvements in the diversity of the civil service during our time in government because steps were being taken to increase their numbers. In NS, hiring managers were encouraged to use diverse selection panels. However, an incident occurred wherein a hiring manager refused to interview two highly qualified candidates because he claimed he couldn't pronounce their names and presumed they couldn't speak English. On the other side, we knew managers who wanted to recruit diverse candidates, but unfortunately, union rules and the extra paperwork required to designate a position as being diverse challenged even the most willing.

The numbers are important and so is the welcome diverse employees receive. We learned of numerous examples of intolerance with result-ing impacts on human resource costs — from reduced productivity to increased turnover. We also recall statistics showing that while the Nova Scotia civil service was successful in recruiting more Indigenous people and persons with disabilities, their associated retention rates were dismal. This was attributed to lack of support and collegiality in their workplace.

On the national front, consider a recent case involving a thank-you video produced by the federal Public Service Commission in which animated bureaucrats are portrayed as all white. It's especially disheartening that those who created this message failed to reflect the diversity of the civil service. It's also troubling that the avatars appear to depict senior management — which underscores a deeper issue.[12]

Other diversity matters requiring attention include data collection and analysis. In many cases, we recall those running programs did not have specific data associated with the populations tapping into their programs and would therefore not know how best to tailor services to meet a variety of needs. It was rare to mine population data available through census data and general social surveys conducted by Statistics Canada to better understand characteristics associated with a diverse citizenry or client base. We have a lot more to say about research in Chapter 8.

During our years of service, efforts to engage with diverse communities on significant policies and services affecting them were also inadequate and this partially related to a lack of outreach efforts, as well as language barriers. There are significant costs associated with undertaking inclusive public engagement. Costs hampered efforts, but we also note a lack of political will to engage.

There were — and still are — offices in place that can help other bureaucrats reach out to diverse communities, but because of government structure many employees may not be aware of them or know how to use their services. In Nova Scotia, the Office of Aboriginal Affairs coordinates efforts with the Mi'kmaq of NS. In some provinces and federally there are also acts governing French-language services. There are additional institutional structures that serve diverse segments of the population; again, in NS, these include African Nova Scotian Affairs, the Accessibility Directorate and Gaelic Affairs.

We hope you now have a better understanding of some key issues that affect the culture of government bureaucracy, including how they can influence the delivery of services and programs. We also hope that managers and leaders throughout the system will contemplate how to

improve the negative implications from the many factors we've identified. This could help challenge perceptions of poor management and
help governments hang on to good employees. Good management can
aid in creating a healthy and productive work culture. Conversely, poor
management can result in a culture that people run away from. As one
senior leader, who prefers to remain anonymous, says about serving the
public, "At the end of the day, what we do affects real people — whether
you are a law maker or answering the phone. If I could have one wish it
would be that everyone in government thought about the people they
served, not the pay cheque they receive, and the security government
brings from an employment perspective."

Case in Point

On more than one occasion we participated in and encouraged our
leaders and colleagues to take the "gorilla" test. We thought it might
be a way for them to recognize that they were so focused on task that
they failed to see what was right in front of them, including negative
impacts on the culture of the organization because of the factors we've
identified in this chapter.

The creators of the test[13] ask readers to:

> Imagine you are asked to watch a short video in which six
> people — three in white shirts and three in black shirts —
> pass basketballs around. While you watch, you must keep a
> silent count of the number of passes made by the people in
> white shirts. At some point, a gorilla strolls into the middle
> of the action, faces the camera and thumps its chest, and
> then leaves, spending nine seconds on screen. Would you
> see the gorilla?
>
> Almost everyone has the intuition that the answer is
> 'Yes, of course I would.' How could something so obvious
> go completely unnoticed? But when we did this experi-
> ment at Harvard University several years ago, we found
> that half of the people who watched the video and counted

the passes missed the gorilla. It was as though the gorilla was invisible.

This experiment reveals two things: that we are missing a lot of what goes on around us, and that we have no idea that we are missing so much. To our surprise, it has become one of the best-known experiments in psychology.

We played this for many colleagues and recall several instances where people thought we had used two separate videos; they simply couldn't believe they would miss something so obvious. The experiment did little to change the behaviour of those we were trying to influence, but at least we can say we tried.

In the context of workplace culture, it is imperative that people see what is going on around them. Once they are aware, they can address those issues that are harming the work environment and introduce or build on those that are making a positive contribution. This exercise demonstrates how easy it is to miss what is right in front of you.

TALKING POINTS
- Recognize that bureaucratic culture — like all cultures — is not dictated, but rather it is shaped by many factors including structure and control systems within the organization.
- Silos and chains of command are an inherent part of government structure, so people need to find ways to work within their constraints.
- When faced with political grandstanding about cutting the public service, bureaucrats should keep their heads up high and continue to demonstrate the value of the work being performed.
- Unions are necessary and powerful, and while they more often make a valuable contribution to the workplace, there are times when they can make a bad situation worse.
- Political hires may breed resentment, but bureaucrats can take comfort knowing many such hires won't be around for the long haul.
- Ongoing discussions about values and ethics are worthy endeavours, as are investments in training and development.

- Transformational change is rare in the public sector; admitting this is an important step in setting expectations for change.
- Everyone should look for ways to be more inclusive and recognize the value that diversity adds to workplaces.
- It was said that employees don't generally leave a job because of the pay, but rather they leave because of poor management practices; managers may want to keep that in mind and work to improve ineffective practices so they can keep effective employees.

Don't take our word for it

With all the negativity present, we did want to flag a July 2017 article in the *Ottawa Citizen* that reports:

> Canada's public service is the most effective in the world, according to the results of a new British study that compares the performance of government workforces in 31 countries. Canada topped the rankings based on its overall score for performance measures such as tax administration, policy making, inclusiveness, openness, integrity, crisis management, fiscal and financial management. New Zealand, Australia and the United Kingdom were also among the top ten. The survey represented the first-ever attempt to compare bureaucracies worldwide.[14]

Chapter 3

FROM THE INSIDE AND OUT – MANAGING A MINEFIELD OF RELATIONSHIPS

"Minister, I have warned you before about the dangers of talking to people in the Department. I implore you to stay out of the minefield of local government. It is a political graveyard!"

— Sir Humphrey Appleby, *Yes Minister*

IN THIS CHAPTER:
- Relationships to Navigate on the Political Side of the House
- Relationships to Build and Maintain within the Bureaucracy
- Interactions with External Groups, including the General Public
- Challenges and Constraints That Interfere with Relationship Building

Given the stereotypical views of bureaucrats, it's not a stretch to believe that some assume bureaucrats have no personalities and thus lack the ability to develop relationships. Chances are many of you have had a negative encounter with a bureaucrat, so you likely want to avoid them.

Unfortunately, bureaucrats cannot do the same. They have to manage a minefield of relationships to do their jobs well. Depending on the purpose of the interaction, bureaucrats across the country have to assume various roles, ranging from supporters, mediators and conciliators to babysitters, influencers and, yes, dictators.

We recognize relationship management can be a challenging aspect of the job in any organization, but there are dynamics in all governments that make it even more complicated and, at times, more difficult. To help you better understand those dynamics, we're focusing this chapter on the various players within the system and highlighting some of our interactions with them. We'll also dig deeper into relationships bureaucrats work to build and maintain with stakeholders and the general public on the governments' behalf. We'll conclude with a look at issues that can influence or constrain how bureaucrats interact with members of the public. We hope you'll better appreciate the layers of power within government and the bureaucracy and the extent of the networking required to get work done, especially on a national level. Of course, the groups we identify can also hold things up. All of these relationships directly affect how bureaucrats feel about their work environment and their interactions with colleagues, stakeholders and the general public.

Relationships to Navigate on the Political Side of the House

We start this exploration of government relationships with the players on the political side of the house. These people are always coming and going; most relationships are fleeting, to say the least. Still, while these political players are in their positions, they exert a great deal of influence over the bureaucracy, including setting the tone for interactions.

Ministers

We begin with ministers. Before you compare a minister with a chief executive officer (CEO) of an organization, you'll want to be aware of some significant differences. First and foremost, unlike a CEO, ministers have no direct authority over the people below them. This role falls to deputy ministers, who are governed by legislation and bound by collective agreements pertaining to the civil service. It's also fair to say that some ministers come into a department with little or no knowledge of the work they are expected to oversee. In those cases, many employees are required to step up and fill in the skill and knowledge gaps. This arrangement can lead to frustration, resentment and overworked employees. However, if bureaucrats are lucky enough to get a strong minister, it can have a positive impact on how they feel about and do their jobs.

Of course, unless a bureaucrat is in a head office environment, chances are they will not have an opportunity to develop a relationship with their minister, given the relatively short tenure of elected officials. We know some bureaucrats who never met a minister during careers that spanned decades. This is especially true at the federal level, as employees are spread throughout the country, while politicians and senior officials generally reside in Ottawa. On the other hand, bureaucrats working in areas such as communications, policy and legal services have frequent contact — sometimes daily, in the case of communications — and a great deal of influence depending on the health of the relationships between key staff and ministers.

We both had wonderful experiences with ministers of all political stripes who respected bureaucrats and their work. We were proud to serve them as confidants, advisors and gatekeepers. Sadly, this was not always the case. Some ministers were arrogant, disrespectful or simply incompetent. That's when we had to dig deep to establish a relationship in the interest of ensuring departmental work was protected, that the department was not embarrassed and, in some cases, that staff were shielded.

The senior bureaucrats we dealt with were adept at quickly assessing a new minister and determining what role they needed to take on, including finding ways to perform their role without offending the minister. This could be tricky, as occasionally, this role was nothing more than babysitting.

In an extreme example, one of us had to travel halfway around the world with the minister to ensure she didn't embarrass the province or department. Our role was to accompany her to all meetings and social activities with the intent of intervening in conversations if we saw them going down a path that could be either inappropriate or embarrassing for the province. Some may have welcomed this opportunity. However, the trip occurred over a holiday period; the flight was twenty-four hours long; and the trip itself was very short, making it difficult to adjust to significant time changes. This minister also had no respect for bureaucrats; spending time with her to simply monitor what might be said felt like a punishment. It was also hard to accept that significant resources, time and money were spent simply because the minister had to be babysat.

In another instance, one of us got a big dose of disrespect while briefing a new minister. He read his newspaper and ate his breakfast during the briefing, demonstrating complete disinterest in what we had to say. When we paused to make a point, he would eventually look up and the briefing would continue; he would then immediately get back to his paper and meal. This happened several times, until he cut the briefing short. The bulk of the content that employees took hours to prepare was never presented, and he asked no questions. We would later learn he was dissatisfied that the premier of the day assigned him to what he considered a low-profile department. We figured it was easier for him to show his unhappiness to bureaucrats rather than to raise it with the premier. The incident set the relationship with the people in the room off to a bad start, and the disrespect shown prevented a solid, healthy relationship from ever forming.

One of us also had to call out a minister for intimidating behaviour. He had called our home after work hours to complain about a rumour that we said he was an insignificant minister. When he refused to disclose the name of the person who shared the rumour, we ended the conversation with a goodbye and a *click*. Admittedly, it was a sleepless night. We worried about possible fallout the next day. It was later revealed he was upset with the department because one of his friends was impacted by layoffs that he believed we had a role in. He wanted to throw his weight around and blow off some steam, but he had no right to do what he did, and respectfully standing our ground was warranted. You can imagine this made for uncomfortable and tense interactions for some time after.

Thankfully, incidents like this were few and far between. Most of the time we were given many opportunities to engage with ministers, including sharing the results of our research and analysis on dozens of issues affecting the organization and the citizenry; exploring options for response; and preparing ministers for discussions and debates in the house, in the media and at countless meetings with stakeholders and members of the public. It was often a high-pressure environment with fast turnaround times and a lot at stake — for the minister and for us. Ministers play a key role in setting the tone, and we found that when we had good relationships with ministers, that translated into positive relationships with others, including our colleagues and the people we served. We tried harder because they, too, were engaged and cared about the work of the department.

Executive assistants and political appointments

We now turn our attention to political appointees. We dealt most often with ministerial executive assistants (EAs), but there were rare occasions when political staff from the premier's office attended meetings on controversial issues. Governing parties of all sorts appoint these political staffers. We liked to think of these people as short-term tenants; they were never around for long, so most employees didn't invest much time developing strong relationships with them. EAs are party faithfuls: they serve department ministers and may have helped them win their seat. Most times, they are simply appointed to these contract positions and are not considered civil servants, which mean they come and go as the ministers or parties change.

We were taught that an EA's job is to assist the minister with their needs concerning the department and to respond to, and run interference for, constituents and ridings. They have no official power, but they do have direct and easy access to the minister and deputy minister. Because of this, we were always mindful to tread carefully as they could make life difficult. We noticed it took a while for EAs to find their footing in departments, with some initially trying to direct or critique the work of bureaucrats. There was one instance where an EA would constantly barge into our office, demand something be done, or that he be given sensitive information he was not entitled to have. Our only recourse was to ensure the deputy minister was aware of his requests and to have her intervene and continue to educate the individual on the inappropriateness of his actions. She was there to remind him that bureaucrats do not report to him in any fashion.

Because EAs are responsible for addressing concerns or issues arising from a minister's constituency, we were often required to pay special attention to such requests. Sometimes people in constituencies wanted favours and hoped political interference would get them what they wanted. These situations had to be carefully managed, because while the ministers and EAs expected resolution, we had rules to follow. More often than not, we had to deny their requests. There were no winners in these situations, and we were often the labelled the bad guys, resulting in unnecessary strain on relationships.

We discussed political hires in Chapter 2, but we wanted to share another example here because of the impact it had on relationships. In this case, someone with close ties to the party in power went through a competitive job process but failed to get an entry-level research position in a department. Two weeks later, she was appointed as the deputy minister of that same department! Her interactions with the employees who turned her down were tense, to say the least, and it made for a difficult first year. Bureaucrats in this department had to dig deep and draw on their interpersonal skills to get over the awkwardness and resentment felt on both sides.

We'll conclude this look at political staff with one more observation. Towards the end of our career, we noticed many EAs attempting to intervene into departmental business, including attempting to push ideological perspectives on policy positions. Sometimes the conversations were uncomfortable, and we recall one in particular where an EA attempted to discuss abortion rights, which was outside of the department's mandate and not on the table for discussion period. This challenged the relationship, to say the least.

Committees of the house

Moving beyond departmental political players, it was rare for us to interact with politicians serving on various legislative committees. Those interactions were usually reserved for the top layers in the bureaucratic chain of command. One of the more prominent house committees in most legislatures is public accounts, which is one of the few places where elected officials get to question bureaucrats about government work in a public setting. Most bureaucrats will tell you that appearing before public accounts is not pleasant. While the intentions behind politicians participating in this process may be honourable, these committees were often used to score political points using the bureaucrats who appear before them as pawns. We lost sleep when we were involved in appearances before these committees because of the work required to prepare and the discomfort knowing shots would be fired. We made sure we did our homework beforehand, including trying to anticipate where the questioning would lead and briefing the minister on controversial issues that were guaranteed to come to light. From our vantage point, appearances before these committees do little to enhance relationships because of the adversarial environment and the wish to score political points.

Despite the games played by all sides while participating in committees of the house, these processes provide a check on the governing party, giving opposition members opportunities to challenge government policies and spending. With COVID-19 disruptions, these processes were placed on the backburner. Nova Scotia's premier came under fire for delaying their restart.

Another committee that some bureaucrats encountered dealt with law amendments. This is the group of elected politicians who listen to public feedback on bills introduced in the house. It's been our experience that most who speak are opposed to something or other; you will likely find many bureaucrats sitting in the room monitoring the issues being raised and preparing responses for the minister. The opposition has their people in the room, and the media is guaranteed to fuel any controversies that do arise. Again, given the political grandstanding that follows these appearances, relationships become strained on all sides.

Opposition members

And speaking of the opposition, if bureaucrats are in the civil service for any length of time, it is likely members of the opposition will become part of a future governing party. We always kept that in mind when interacting with an opposition member, as we knew that they could one day be our minister. We didn't want to do anything that would jeopardize future interactions.

We recall one incident where a former colleague used the word "ignorant" — as in not knowing the facts — to describe an opposition member's comments about an issue that garnered some press. That member eventually became the minister of the department where the colleague worked, and recalling that conversation made for some awkward moments.

Even without such awkward exchanges, it can be difficult to form relationships with members of a new government, particularly at provincial and federal levels, because many come into their roles with distrust of the bureaucracy. Many may not be aware that most bureaucrats take principles associated with public service seriously, which, as we noted in Chapter 1, includes non-partisan advice. That initial distrust translated into disrespect and delays in securing decisions, as well as exclusion and secrecy. Because ministers can influence the tone in a department, these negative interactions trickle down into all layers of the organization, ultimately influencing workplace culture and how bureaucrats interact with their peers and the general public.

Relationships to Build and Maintain within the Bureaucracy

Switching to the bureaucratic side of the government workplace, there is a long list of individuals and groups any bureaucrat has to interact with to get the information needed to do the job; to secure the necessary resources to carry out tasks; or to get approval to proceed with an initiative or project.

Senior officials committees

We'll start with the top of the hierarchy. While we served, there were groups of high-ranking bureaucrats — mainly at the deputy ministers' level — who were on social and economic policy committees. One of their major roles was to vet proposals that had implications across portfolios before the proposals could make their way to cabinet. The people who served on these committees had a lot of power and decision-making authority. They could easily put the kibosh to initiatives. It was sometimes difficult to maintain relationships with the people on these committees because there was high turnover, as people often changed positions or departments. People who served at these tables also had varying degrees of knowledge. Some had egos, which added layers of complexity to relationship management. We did learn to take presentations to these groups seriously and spent countless hours preparing when we were lucky enough to get a slot on one of their agendas. Getting a sign-off at that table represented significant endorsement for the work, so every effort was made to be respectful and professional no matter what curveballs were thrown.

We're going to include high-profile transition teams in this group as well, although you can argue they are a hybrid as some include both bureaucrats and members of key stakeholder groups. We recall several such groups being formed following major economic disruptions, where top-ranking bureaucrats joined with key stakeholders to assess options for response. A recent example in Nova Scotia was the transition team announced to help the forestry sector following the winding down of the Northern Pulp mill, which was being led by a deputy minister. The team experienced a relationship bump early on, following the removal of an industry member who reportedly was advocating for options that would see the mill continue. This was not part of the transition team's mandate. News outlets reported he was gone from the transition team. We imagine this had a negative ripple effect on the relationship between the committee and other members of the industry.

Working groups and task teams
Often times, senior officials suggested that working groups or task teams be struck to undertake more work on an issue. While slow to get things done, we recognized they were necessary to accomplish work that cut across many departments. Unfortunately, our relationships within these groups were hampered by turf issues, including conflicts

with theoretical or ideological frames of reference; lack of time for departmental representatives to participate; limited resources or lack of willingness to share resources; and hesitancy associated with showing departmental cards early or not being given permission to share departmental thinking, especially on controversial or costly issues. Additional factors that challenged the best relationships included deadline pressure, political interference and public scrutiny. They also tended to be closed shops. We recall fighting to get diverse voices included at some of these tables. All of these issues impede the work to be done, often leaving people frustrated, wishing they had never been appointed to the committee and dreading the next meeting.

Other collegial relationships

Other colleagues critical to getting any work done in government include bureaucrats in central support units such as finance, human resources and information technology. These relationships had to be fostered, but we — when we were staff within these central agencies — experienced divided loyalties when our own departmental policies conflicted with the departments we were expected to serve. One example that speaks to divided loyalties involved pending layoffs. The central corporate body responsible for human resources (HR) had not, and stated they would not, be implementing any information sessions for staff regarding what to expect. Consequently, the department facing the layoffs went ahead and hosted an educational session for staff. The corporate body, however, was unhappy with us going forward alone. This resulted in complaints to our supervisor, who let us know they did not see us as good team players. The problem boiled down to two deputy ministers — one in the central HR shop and the other in the department facing the layoffs — who had differing ideas on how they wanted things done. We actually reported to both, so we found ourselves taking action that we knew would please one and annoy the other.

Within departments, there are employees in legal services, policy and communications who can ease the load or add to it. We tried to get to know them as individuals, as well as understand their processes, information needs and challenges, with hopes of paving the way to healthy working relationships.

Staff at the centre of government are also important to mention, especially because they are closest to political leaders. Many of the people in these offices thought they ran the show, and for the most part, they did. The mandate and responsibility of central policy shops are to drive the political agenda, and they do that without direct authority over the civil service. Even without formal authority, we worked hard to build relationships with staff in these offices, as they drove the paperwork — for which we were tasked with preparing — that made its way to decision makers.

Stepping beyond departmental and provincial borders, it is also worth noting that many bureaucrats have to build relationships with people who sit at federal/provincial/territorial (FPT) tables. There are dozens and dozens of these groups. Such groups often get their mandates and marching orders from official communiqués emanating from ministerial and deputy ministerial discussions.

We participated in many of these over the years and saw how the relationships we had built with our peers paid off. We were able to call on them for help, which included getting data, tips and names of others to speak to about an issue or project. While working on service dog certification, for example, one of us was able to reach out to colleagues in British Columbia who had already gone down a similar path. They freely shared information on their licence regime and administrative structure and gave Nova Scotia permission to use their service dog assessment tool. We also had opportunities to share knowledge that informed policies affecting the whole country.

We've highlighted the more prominent groups of players within the bureaucracy, but there are other relationships that have to be nurtured, including those with immediate bosses, others in the chain of command and colleagues within a bureaucrat's own unit or division.

Interactions with External Groups, including the General Public

Early on, we mentioned that some people we knew entered the public service because they wanted to work for the public good, including making positive contributions to civic life and helping society's most vulnerable. After some of the less-than-civil experiences bureaucrats regularly face, we can't help but wonder how many would want the job in the first place; were they aware of the negative interactions they would suffer? Engaging with the public made for some great moments, but also ended in some of our worst.

We've had hundreds of encounters with organizational representatives and individual members of the public over the years. We often felt privileged to help many people connect with government programs and services, including responding to a multitude of information and service requests; making the case for system responses; and gathering feedback on ways to improve processes.

While the majority of our encounters were professional, others were strained at best and hostile at worst. This, of course, made navigating relationships difficult. Many didn't care who we were and what job we held. To them, we were the face of the government and they treated us as though we were elected officials. One of us was once repeatedly criticized for the government's lack of action on an advocacy organization's wish list. In one particularly aggressive callout, another person at the table suggested we were paid for the abuse, so we should "suck it up." This came from people we were trying to help move their agenda forward. Tears of frustration were shed after that nasty exchange; we really did have no choice but to take it. The relationship suffered as a result.

Some members of the public also treat bureaucrats with disdain, especially when they have no choice but to deal with government. As examples, someone paying a fine will likely resent the bureaucrat processing the payment. Consider, too, the individual who has been denied a student loan and is understandably upset, as it means they cannot attend university. When faced with similar situations, we tried to empathize with those we were dealing with, but there were many times individuals made it very difficult to want to help them.

One of us had to tell a member of the public she was not qualified for a role in government that she wanted. This news did not sit well with her and for months, she would call, leaving rude and threatening messages. Finally, she threatened that she was going to have her son-in-law "visit" when he got out of prison, and we would be sorry that we didn't give her a job. We knew then there were mental health issues at play. We hesitated to bring law enforcement into the picture, but at that point, we had no choice. Thankfully, after a visit from the police, the calls stopped.

In a few cases, we did receive permission to cut off contact from abusive people, but the majority of the time we had to take it on the chin. This was especially true of relationships with stakeholder groups, where we worked hard to develop respectful interactions. One of us was especially challenged on this front early in our career, when upon entering a boardroom filled with members of a joint industry-government committee, the chair asked if we were there to jump out of a cake. We doubt something like that would happen today; if it did, there could be consequences for the perpetrator.

Over the years, many of our friends suggested the personal attacks or public criticism were all part of the job and to basically let them slide because of the "good benefits" public servants enjoy. We never believed this. We felt that if we gave respect, we also deserved it. There were too many occasions to count wherein we had to bite our tongues, take a deep breath and swallow a snarky response to silence a critic. While we knew it would give us short-term pleasure, we also knew it wasn't the right thing to do. We, like many bureaucrats, wanted to build good relationships so that we could provide the best service for citizens. This may sound corny, but it is true.

We do understand that not everybody agrees with the decisions governments make. However, we were always dismayed when members of the public felt it was within their right to abuse bureaucrats who were only carrying out orders. We recall one instance where we were badmouthed in the press and blamed for shutting down an arts council. We have more to say about this experience in Chapter 5, but for now we want to call out an advocate for the organization, who took our pictures and threatened to distribute them, claiming then everyone would know who was to blame. This individual knew the government made the decision, and we were simply trying to pick up the pieces and do our best to support the individuals affected with compassion and respect.

Despite these negative encounters, we think advocates are critical and play a key role in shaping government policy, programs and services. While most bureaucrats do not directly interact with advocates, those who work in policy, communications or a department that focuses on social issues will benefit from understanding the roles and positions of advocacy groups and look for ways to build positive relationships with them.

Despite those who lump advocates together with lobbyists, we think it is important that bureaucrats recognize their differences. Both involve efforts to influence public policy and laws, but the methods these groups use differ. The relationships bureaucrats establish with representatives should reflect those differences.

Lobbyists are usually well-funded, more brazen and focused on a narrow set of interests, usually economic in scope. During our years of service, the more sophisticated groups often surveyed all parties before an election, where those running said how they would address the group's particular pet projects. Thankfully, parties started to treat these more seriously over the years with non-committal responses while running for election. We knew such groups had lots of power, including direct access to the highest levels of government. We were reminded of this during one of our classes at Dalhousie University, where an invited guest speaker and leader of a powerful business lobby group bragged about having breakfast meetings with the premier of the day every Monday morning. We recall shaking our heads at the time. For a lobbyist to crow about skirting around bureaucrats to a room full of them lacked judgement.

It's been our experience that advocacy groups tend to be associated with not-for-profit initiatives that are social or environmental in scope and with broader public good goals at the heart of their efforts. If you happen to fall into either the lobbyist or advocacy camp, we do recommend working with bureaucrats first and not last. You may face resistance either way, but a scorned bureaucrat can throw lots of curveballs.

Challenges and Constraints That Interfere with Relationship Building

We've identified the many relationships that bureaucrats navigate as they go about their work. We now want to explore some of the challenges that can interfere with the ability to develop positive relationships with others.

1. Confidentiality requirements

One of the biggest challenges relates to confidentiality requirements. When it comes to building healthy relationships, principles such as honesty, transparency and knowledge-sharing are highly valued. However, as a bureaucrat, there are limits. Confidentiality requirements definitely interfered with our ability to develop constructive relationships — some of which were fraught with tension and competing interests. We were put on the spot on more than one occasion because the people we were dealing with knew we had more information, but we couldn't share it with them. This rubbed up against personal values associated with wanting to be forthright and honest. These conflicts were unavoidable, and whenever we encountered a confidentiality issue, we tried to explain those constraints.

2. Directed to act contrary to what people want

We occasionally found ourselves in situations that we didn't control, and where our role was often dictated by those above us. Tilly Pillay, who spent nearly two decades in senior leadership roles with government and since 2017 serves as an executive director with the Nova Scotia Barristers' Society, shared the following observation with us: "At the macro level, staff, deputies and politicians all have different views about particular situations, and you can't throw politicians under the bus when you are directed to take a particular course of action." To get through these challenges, we tried to explain our piece of the work, including outlining our limitations in terms of what we could do. We also tried to be honest and that included recognizing that agreement was not always possible.

3. Pressure to protect political interests

Bureaucrats also face pressure from their political leaders to toe the party line. Aucoin, in a 2012 journal article titled "New Political Governance in Westminster Systems: Impartial Public Administration and Management Performance at Risk," states: "There has also been an explosion of organized interest groups, advocacy groups, lobbyists, and think tanks (partisan and independent, but increasingly the former). Political parties are still the primary political organizations insofar as they compete for and hold office, but they now share the very crowded political arena with a multiplicity of other political organizations. The political pressures on the public service are increased as ministers expect public servants to protect ministerial interests in their interactions with these groups and other opinion leaders, especially when conducted in open consultative forums. Governments expect what they regard as *their* public servants to promote their agenda in the conduct of their activities, notwithstanding the fact that a government's agenda is necessarily a partisan agenda." Aucoin further notes that: "To the extent that the public service is expected to communicate the government's message in ways that advance or defend its merits, impartiality is undermined."[1]

4. Inability to disclose biases and agendas upfront

We encouraged leaders to state their biases up front because engagement is rarely undertaken without specific objectives in mind. On occasion, these biases were not stated on purpose. We think it is highly unlikely that any government is ever interested in sharing power associated with a decision; chances are any engagement or consultation exercise focuses on information gathering or persuasion. If a decision had been made, we tried to encourage leaders to own it. In our experience, governments underestimate how much the public knows. Citizens have grown wary of government engagement efforts because, too often, the effort was for show and not substance. This practice can breed resentment and questions regarding the credibility of legitimate engagement practices and relationships have suffered as a result.

5. Difficulties establishing boundaries

Another challenge when interacting with others involves establishing boundaries. We often found it was inherently difficult to establish boundaries to focus on one issue at a time. So much of what governments do are inextricably linked to other issues, and when bureaucrats set out to deal with one issue it often led to others. We found it hard to stay focused and avoid the rabbit holes that could have sucked us underground.

As an example, when consulting with employees about a new hiring policy, we were constantly being asked to address individual concerns about matters not related to the issue at hand. It was difficult to push back, as we knew the other issues mattered to people in the room as well. However, to be respectful to those who came to offer thoughts on the new policy and ensure we had the information we needed, we had to constantly remind people why we were there.

This type of interaction creates challenges for relationships because of the friction that results from trying to bring the focus back to the original issue. In these cases, we were accused of not listening, not caring and not able to handle more than one thing at a time. It's not hard to see how relationships can quickly become adversarial in these situations.

6. Talk is not cheap

Another issue plaguing relationship development is the time and resources required to build relationships with individuals and groups, which governments often underestimate. This includes hosting meetings and preparing materials necessary to support engagement and consultation. During our time in government, rarely were appropriate people, resources or financial resources assigned to the work. And it was just as rare to see a line item in a project budget referencing "consultation or engagement" or an associated action item in the list of deliverables. Of course, governments eventually pay a price if they don't communicate. It demonstrates a "we know better than you" attitude, which understandably leads to cynicism and can turn potential supporters into vocal critics.

7. Mystifying processes

Another challenge is the perception that the bureaucracy is impenetrable. We tried hard to explain the processes in our dealings with external groups. We also advocated for including external people in the process wherever possible. Of course, that, too, came with risks. Some leaders genuinely believed they knew the answer to a specific problem or issue, so did not feel the need to include people from outside. We also know that some people figure there is no point trying to work their way into a relationship that may help their cause because they find the organization too big, too complex and has what seems like barriers at every door. Unfortunately, we believe many people have given up trying to work with governments or public servants. That resulted in a lack of engagement in the entire democratic process.

We trust you now have a better appreciation of the minefield of relationships bureaucrats have to navigate, as well as the constraints that can hamper interactions. Just as we tried to empathize when dealing with the public, we hope readers can do the same when dealing with bureaucrats and perhaps even cut them a bit of slack when facing frustrating interactions.

Case in Point

For this case study, we share details on the effort that went into building and maintaining relationships to help move a controversial initiative forward. One of us was directly involved in a joint project between the Department of Justice and the Nova Scotia Government Employees Union, where both the deputy minister of justice and the president of the union agreed to work together to implement a new model of supervision at Nova Scotia's largest correctional facility.

Evidence showed that direct supervision was considered a better model than the remote supervision underway at the jail. With the new model, staff would be stationed inside the living units and not separated from offenders by physical barriers, as was the case at the time. This would allow staff to maintain direct and frequent contact with offenders in their work area and use the interaction to build effective relationships and manage offender behaviour. Jurisdictions using the model reported numerous benefits, including reduced assaults; fewer complaints; quieter and cleaner living spaces; and improved employee morale.

To engage as many people as possible in the planning effort, three levels of joint activity were structured, with a steering committee providing oversight, another group overseeing implementation and a third identifying actions required if the initiative was to get off the ground. The steering committee included the deputy minister and union president, along with senior staff from the correctional centre and representatives from the provincial Ombudsman's Office, and Labour and Workforce Development, as well as advocacy representatives from the John Howard Society and the Elizabeth Fry Society. The implementation group included management and union representatives, as did the third group who were focused on actions.

Evidence was gathered to inform all planning participants, including data on offender and employee demographics; public opinion research on perceptions regarding the performance of the prison system; results of interviews with a mix of management, union and advocacy groups about their views on the existing environment, and hopes and fears associated with the new model. To say the relationships were strained would be an understatement. Many spoke of barriers across and between groups, including barriers between correctional officers and offenders, as well as barriers between supervisors and those on the front line. The environment was described as high-stress and high-tension run by a para-military command and control culture. There was a lot of staff turnover and sick leave within the facility as well. Almost everyone referenced fear in one form or another — fear of offenders; fear of safety; fear of change; and fear of management discipline. People also spoke about a high level of mistrust across and between all levels of the organization — of management, of the department, of the labour board, of the Ombudsman. This was combined with a multi-dimensional "us versus them" mentality — between officers and offenders; between groups of offenders; between supervisors and officers; and between management and staff.

One aspect everybody agreed on was that the status quo wasn't working and all had a duty to make it better. It took many, many months and dozens of meetings to build the relationships needed to undertake the work jointly. It took many more months to actually do the work, including training staff; instituting safety and security features; making physical changes to the space; introducing incentives for offender compliance; and developing new standard operating procedures. The initiative was finally launched in one area of the prison — thanks to many people who stuck out their necks because they believed the model was a more humane response to improve safety and dignity, and an opportunity to interact in a positive way that could support offenders' rehabilitation.

In this case, the processes created space for relationships to develop. Without those relationships, the initiative may never have gotten off the ground.

TALKING POINTS

- Bureaucrats have to manage a multitude of relationships — some of which are riddled with tension and mistrust.
- Many of the relationships bureaucrats work to establish are relatively fleeting given the short- term tenure of political leaders and their staff.
- Bureaucrats shouldn't underestimate the power of good relationships — especially those with colleagues — in helping them serve the public good.
- Good relationships take work. They don't just happen.
- When dealing with the public, bureaucrats are the face of government, and they have no choice but to take the good with the bad.
- When fostering or negotiating relationships, bureaucrats need to recognize their limitations and power.
- No matter a bureaucrat's opinion, they work for government, not a specific advocacy or lobby group.
- While worth every effort, working to develop and maintain relationships is not for the faint of heart, as there are many issues that get in the way.

Don't take our word for it

We'll conclude this chapter with some words of wisdom for bureaucrats from a former colleague, who served for decades at both the departmental and central government agency level. She says:

> Be nice to people. I am not saying this just because it's the right thing to do. As daunting as it first seems, the service is really a very tiny ecosystem. And if you move around, which is kinda fun, the same people will roll in and out of your life in different roles. The guy or girl you jump on today might be your boss in a few years — one with a really good memory. Even if this was not the case, the person you jumped is now totally preoccupied with the event and, through osmosis, everyone else in that unit is caught up in a great big mess of miserable inefficiency, which can last days or even weeks. I always thought it would be interesting, if not frightening, to measure that in terms of lost productivity. You can have an amazing and extremely rewarding career as a bureaucrat with the added bonus of making life-long friends. Why make it less so by fighting a system that will not and, probably should not, change.

Chapter 4
BEST-LAID PLANS

"Politicians like to panic, they need activity. It's their substitute for achievement."

— Sir Humphrey Appleby, *Yes Minister*

IN THIS CHAPTER:

- Changing Tires on a Moving Car: The Planning Context within Government
- Vested Interests: A Look at Who Has the Most to Gain from Planning Exercises
- What's Old Is New Again: Planning Trends and Influences
- Myriad Government Planning Processes and Products
- Reality Checks Associated with Planning in Government Environments
- Why Bother with Planning, Given All the Challenges?

We are well aware of the stereotypical image of bureaucrats as paper-pushers. We agree there is much truth to that because, as citizens, we have dealt with the burden of bureaucratic paperwork. Just because we worked for the government didn't meant we could escape filling out required documents, waiting for a response or shuffling off to a government office to wait our turn or for our number to be called when accessing services we needed or wanted.

We shake our heads at times when we realize how much paperwork can be involved in one government transaction. However, we are a bit more forgiving, because we know first-hand that paperwork issued to citizens often arises from the many checks and balances needed to satisfy legislative and regulatory requirements governing programs and services.

When it comes to administering paperwork issued to citizens, most bureaucrats have little choice but to chase the paper trail in their efforts to serve the public. The fear of a file review by ever-present auditor generals' offices is enough to make the laxest bureaucrat dot every "i" and cross every "t."

Bureaucrats also have little choice when it comes to dealing with internally generated paperwork, and the burden is especially heavy in the planning realm.

We expect most know that governments usually have extensive plans in place to deal with critical incidents, such as weather-related emergencies, potentially catastrophic events and, as we experienced in 2020, pandemics. But many people may be surprised to learn that all levels of government have plans for just about everything they do, including at the corporate, departmental, program, service, issue and individual performance level.

We're devoting a chapter to government planning processes because they can be complex and somewhat daunting. They eat up a great deal of time and resources, resulting in endless to-do lists for bureaucrats. We share some thoughts on why planning is important, as well as examine who has a vested interest in these exercises. We also explore various ideologies that have influenced planning initiatives before identifying the myriad of planning processes and products produced by bureaucrats. We conclude this chapter with some reality checks on why planning is especially difficult in government. After reading this, we hope you'll better appreciate why planning documents, which can take years to develop, are often shelved both figuratively and literally, something that is difficult for many to wrap their heads around.

Putting our citizen hats on, we are comforted knowing that some people are thinking about where governing needs to go to address the issues that society faces on an ongoing basis. However, as bureaucrats, we know plans can be derailed in government. Just like any other institution, government cannot predict the future, and things inevitably get in the way of the work required to execute the plans. COVID-19 was a jarring reminder of that. We think incrementalism — defined as the science of muddling through — is a more useful description of the reality bureaucrats face when working through these processes.

Changing Tires on a Moving Car: The Planning Context within Government

We were two of thousands of bureaucrats across Canada involved in planning processes for various levels of governments, and the numbers have grown significantly over the years. In part, this is because the formalization of planning in government is a relatively new activity for bureaucrats. It emerged from demands by politicians and businesses urging governments to conduct themselves in a more business-like fashion.

Business planning exercises in government took off in the 1990s, replacing those elusive departmental annual reports. While these reports did provide some value, they focused on the years past, with little acknowledgement of plans for the future. Business planning exercises necessitated that government departments look ahead and plan priorities, goals and activities for the coming year.

This was revolutionary in government circles. Leaders must have believed there was little capacity internally to manage this change, as consultants were hired throughout the land to rally the troops and help employees develop and implement business plans. We recall employees from all layers of the organization being ushered into conference rooms for planning sessions. Such exercises were happening across the country, with price tags easily running in the millions of dollars.

Many of our colleagues thought the exercises were a waste of public money, especially in an era of cutbacks. At the time, one colleague in transportation said the department would be better off using the money being spent on consultants to pay for snowplows. All the talk of knowing where you're going is great, but without snowplows, you aren't going to get there in the winter, he deadpanned.

Nova Scotia was just one of the provinces dealing with these new ways of planning and reporting. We recall Alberta and Ontario being hailed as leaders in planning reform efforts. Those of us involved in planning scrambled to get our hands on their documents to borrow language to feed the appetite for similar paperwork. Ireland was also touted as a beacon of reform after it received a major infusion of foreign investment. We poured through their documents and reached out to people within their bureaucracy for words of wisdom. In later years, many in NS looked to Manitoba for guidance because it was known for best practices in areas such as human resources, diversity and inclusion, and had had similar political environments for a number of years.

Bureaucrats who lived through the early days of business planning will no doubt remember several phrases that stick out from business planning proliferation, including the refrain that governments need to learn how to "steer, not row" and that they must "think more like a business." We don't disagree that there are good practices from thinking in this manner, but it was, and is, foolhardy to think governments can simply be run like a commercial business.

Doug Keefe, again, shared the following observation with us: "Unlike business, where profit and losses conclusively demonstrate success or failure, the public interest is vague, subjective, shifting and always controversial. So the public interest in any particular issue is an artificial construct and the best we can do is to say that it is defined by — in descending order — the law, democratic conventions and values, and the directions of publicly accountable officials."

This is not to say governments, like any organization, can't benefit from planning. Theory suggests such exercises are about systematically determining what needs to be done; how things will be done; when things will be done; and what tools and resources are required and available to get things done.

Plans can be used to help people inside and outside an organization understand the goals and directions of the entity, including a department or an elected government. That's particularly important for politicians who want to show the electorate they are involved in actions that will ultimately make society a better place. Bureaucrats also take comfort from plans if they can see where their work fits in the organization, and they can make performance management efforts easier if planned actions are attached to a defined vision or goal. Finally, a good plan can help stakeholders and communities see where they fit in an organization's agenda in the months and even years ahead.

The rationale for planning and its value sounds perfectly reasonable, especially if plans are carried out effectively and meet stated goals. But in government, leaders are often not around long enough to see a plan come to fruition. As a result, they often fail to plan beyond the next election year. With a constant transition of leaders, it is understandable that most new leaders want a plan stamped with their mark. Unfortunately, some elected leaders simply want a new plan to erase the work of the previous government and to feed their egos. Because of that, bureaucrats often have to shelve plans years in the making. Those plans join dozens of others stored in a long-forgotten electronic folder or sit on a shelf, gathering dust.

As former bureaucrats, we hung onto old plans because we knew we would get the opportunity to simply "cut and paste" much of the content from an old plan into a new one. This technique saved time and energy, and reduced the frustrations associated with writing the same thing over and over again.

We say this because when we looked through the pages of old plans, we realized that the significant goals different governments set didn't change much over the years. This is, in part, because governments are trying to fix intractable problems; the supposed new goals looked for the same results. Often, the only major difference in the plans was the introductory remarks from the current leader exclaiming how this plan was going to bring about the changes required to solve age-old dilemmas.

On a lighter note, the other change was the colour of the binder containing the plan. In some of our former departments, plans were grouped into coloured binders: red for Liberal, blue for Tory and orange for NDP. This certainly made it easy to pull out the appropriate binders, depending on which government was embarking on planning sessions.

We acknowledge that shelving or changing a plan mid-stream can make good sense. For instance, when a new government is elected, they rightly expect to see their platform commitments reflected in departmental plans. However, we can recall many instances where we were left shaking our heads and muttering under our breaths about requested changes.

Consider the example of a newly elected government directing employees to abandon — and never again mention — a crime prevention plan that was still underway, and to ditch the promotional materials produced to promote the plan, including perfectly good pens, notepads and T-shirts sporting the plan's tagline. This was done to erase references to the previous government's actions. Unfortunately, this is par for the course. Governments can't resist the urge to view what they inherit from a previous government as faulty and in need of change. Consider what happened south of the border beginning in 2016, with President Trump doing his best to erase as much as he could of former President Obama's work.

Closer to home, planning efforts by our colleagues from across the system to address the enduring social issue of domestic violence were put on the back burner after sexual assault, an equally pervasive social problem, became the issue of the day. The momentum that had been building across the system to tackle domestic violence was lost, and some initiatives in the works were dropped, including a multi-year, multi-agency research project that was gaining traction. There's no question governments have a right to prioritize their activities, but the work that was being done on a serious issue stalled in favour of another getting more press at the time. Both warranted ongoing attention and action.

In these cases, the amount of money expended was not significant in the grand scheme of things. But projects with big budgets can — and would — also get shelved. This is a lesson one of us learned early on while involved in a communications stint with a firm responsible for overseeing the expansion of subway lines in Toronto in the early 1990s. Despite breaking ground on one of the lines — Eglinton West — the multi-billion-dollar project came to a halt when Mike Harris replaced Bob Rae as premier of Ontario in 1995. The waste of resources and energy astounded us at the time, as we naively thought the provincial government would not throw away all the work that had been done.

A former colleague who worked on the project said he still thinks about it every time he heads up Allen Road and "gets ensnared in the interminable traffic jams as they work toward completion of the station there. From the perspective of today, that project was the right way to go, and things only continued to get worse."

Elected officials aren't the only ones who change things on a whim. Consider the example where a deputy minister we served had all the materials supporting a strategic plan redesigned and reprinted to remove the previous deputy's picture and include her own. This was another case of ego which resulted in allocating additional time and resources. These kinds of changes are not free, nor are they inexpensive. It bothered us as both employees and as citizens, given the blatant abuse of power that served no public purpose. We resented our tax dollars being used for a vanity project. Many employees of that department immediately formed a negative opinion of the new deputy minister because they couldn't believe her ego outweighed good judgement.

Another new deputy minister decided to rework departmental goals — developed after months of engagement with staff and stakeholders — because the wording didn't quite fit with her vision for the department. One can rightly argue it is a leader's prerogative to dictate the work that will be done within their scope of command. However, it was in direct contradiction to the agreed-upon process. It generated cynicism among those who had worked on the initial goals in good faith. The deputy minister missed the opportunity to engage employees, which could have led to more positive relationships, as it would have demonstrated a level of respect to the earlier work and the depth of the bureaucrats' knowledge.

Vested Interests: A Look at Who Has the Most to Gain from Planning Exercises

We've outlined a few reasons why planning can be beneficial, but one might reasonably ask why there is an appetite for planning in government, given the inevitable changes in leadership and the short-term shelf life of such documents. The fact is, some groups have a vested interest in these exercises.

Consider bureaucrats. Many bureaucrats champion these exercises because planning suggests an element of control in an unsteady environment. It's like having a road map: there is a level of comfort in having a bigger picture and seeing where departments and employees fit into that picture. Others have become so invested in planning for planning's sake that they've built careers around the exercises. There are employees in departments in all levels of government who are responsible for coordinating planning activities, including gathering the required information from other bureaucrats throughout the system. We often thought we were spending half our time reporting where we were in our planning activities. There were accountability reports, budget forecasts, briefing notes and logic models, to name a few of the more time-consuming documents that needed to be completed on a monthly, quarterly or annual basis.

We have also known bureaucrats who used departmental planning processes as a way to gain support for much-needed initiatives. Consider the following effort by social justice champion and retired Nova Scotia public servant Sharon Davis-Murdoch. Among her public policy accomplishments was the development of the first Provincial Guidelines for Culturally Competent Primary Health Care in Canada.

She says:

> I basically created the opportunity. I was a senior policy analyst in the Department of Health and Wellness in Primary Healthcare, and it was through years of observation, that while the system was certainly looking at the needs of the majority, it was almost oblivious to the needs of minorities and marginalized people.
>
> There was some work in Canada, particularly an interest in bilingualism and the concerns of the Francophone minorities in Canada. But in the work that I was doing, as early as 1996 when I moved into a public service policy role, I was aware that very little was being done. Virtually no work looked specifically at the needs of other minorities, and the usual ap-

proach was to do things in a one-size-fits-all manner.

For years I was aware of that, and finally when we were going through yet another renewal of the health system, and there was no discussion about or recognition of the needs of minorities, I spoke up. I wanted to know how this could be changed and what needed to happen to address it.

I was reporting at that time to a man whom I respected very much, and he said, 'Well, if you want to do something, write a proposal and let's see what you can come up with.' I did. I proposed The Diversity and Social Inclusion in Primary Healthcare Initiative. To my delight, he thought there was something there and that we could possibly sell it to the senior leadership as the way to go forward as part of the department's priorities.

Taking it forward to the senior leadership was something that I knew was unprecedented. Clear to all public servants is that we are there to serve and do what we are asked to do. Those at the policy level work on files they're asked to work on. We are assigned things. Seldom, if ever, are we given the opportunity to come up with our own work.

When I proposed it to the senior leadership, I was delighted and somewhat surprised that they said, 'Well, you make a good point. This makes sense. Yes, we can see this as part of primary health-care renewal — and you can do this piece.'

It wasn't easy. There was a lot of pushback around the concern that (and this is something that has happened across my career), there was too much emphasis on race. Well, the fact is there had never been any emphasis on race prior to this. To talk about race at all was problematic it seemed to me for some people.

In this case, the provincial health renewal planning process already underway gave Davis-Murdoch the perfect launching pad to undertake work that resulted in her receiving two Nova Scotia Premier's Awards of Excellence.

Yet another group creating or requiring plans are politicians. We believe they gravitate towards them because plans give elected leaders something to point to and boast about. Governments are especially prone to launching system-wide "transformative" plans, even though our experience suggests most of them fall flat. We attribute their failure to the inherent stability of a bureaucratic system and a resulting culture that shuns change. Understandably, many of these kinds of plans have an economic focus because generating economic growth is a preoccupation of governments, especially at the provincial level. In the early to mid-2000s, "prosperity" and "sustainability" plans emerged in NS. Before that it was all about "reinventing government," "government renewal" and "government redesign." Today, the focus tends to be on "innovation and adaptation." Many of these buzzwords came from private-sector initiatives from years past. Governments were, and still are, often playing catch-up with planning styles, initiatives and models.

Some government plans are launched with great fanfare and include everything but the kitchen sink. Columnist and former bureaucrat Jim Vibert pointed this out in an article in NS's provincial newspaper *The Chronicle Herald*, blasting one such plan called "Shift" that was geared towards NS's aging population. He called out government for claiming action on more than 50 items in the plan, some of which were generic programs. He writes: "The Shift progress report is a classic example of a government trying to maximize the political currency it earns by padding its resume with stuff that's connected, but only obliquely, to the matter at hand. It's also unfortunate because the good stuff people are doing to advance the objectives of Shift is all but lost in what amounts to a massive pile of prime government manure."[1]

Politicians are also prone to announcing plans that have not had the benefit of bureaucratic second thought, especially when running for office. Given the adversarial party system, it is highly unlikely that politicians would engage bureaucrats when developing their election platforms to get a sense of whether their plans and promises are reasonable, given the resources required to achieve them. We understand there are limitations to the information that is available, but it's easy to get access to previous budgets, staff numbers and existing pressures and challenges facing government departments. Doing that research could reduce the number of unrealistic, pie-in-the-sky goals presented in an election platform, or at the very least, give pause for thought when suggesting new initiatives.

We often experienced a sinking feeling whenever we read something written by political staff that we knew was impossible to achieve, was only there to appease a special interest or would have significant unintended consequences.

One of us worked for a minister who would sporadically throw out a trial balloon, suggesting the government might consider moving departments from Halifax to outlying areas in an effort to spread the wealth associated with good-paying jobs. Another government went further, introducing a plan that would see programs and jobs within fisheries, justice and tourism move to Shelburne, Cape Breton and Windsor, respectively. While the intentions behind such a move had merit, many bureaucrats believed the main reason was to appease a number of the rural ministers' constituents. The upheaval, turmoil and lost productivity had an overall negative impact on the bottom line. Some of our colleagues' lives were turned upside down because they were not in a position to move their homes and families to keep their jobs. Many believed that government did not consider these employees had spouses with jobs in Halifax; had children already enrolled in schools, sports and other activities; were caregivers to parents; and, sadly, some had children who required health services that were provided by the only children's hospital in Halifax.

Employees with these issues had little choice but to either accept lay-offs or move into a new career. Many were specialists in their field, which meant a huge loss of knowledge in the bureaucracy when a number of them decided to leave. New offices — some could argue they were only duplicate offices — had to be established. There were numerous costs associated with recruitment and hiring new people to fill positions.

The jury is still out on whether the goals associated with such actions were ever realized. However, the government of the day did get to stand

up in front of their rural constituents and boast about the jobs they created in the communities where the offices were established.

The last in our list of groups with a vested interest in planning documents are advocacy and lobby groups. Some go through great effort to show how their particular cause aligns with the words of wisdom found in the plan of the day. Business lobby groups like the Canadian Federation of Independent Business and chambers of commerce are particularly good at infusing their words into government plans, including throne speeches. Getting a nod there is the pinnacle, because in NS all promises in those speeches were noted, numbered and tracked religiously by bureaucrats who had to develop plans to deliver on those promises and regularly report on their progress.

Consider "red tape reduction," which has been a favourite business refrain that has made its way into many government plans. In some cases, red tape can and should be reduced, but it doesn't apply across the board. Bureaucrats need to be ready to respond and challenge the words when what's being inserted into government plans is not in the public interest or could put citizens' well-being in jeopardy.

Water safety regulations and the extreme case of the 2000 water tragedy in Walkerton, Ontario, is an example. Seven people died from drinking water contaminated with E. coli due to falsified water testing results. Following the tragedy, strict water safety regulations were imposed to prevent this type of disaster happening again. Fast-forward a decade, and groups started clamouring for a reduction in the red tape that was purposely set up to avoid such a tragedy.

The groups we've just identified have an obvious interest in government planning processes. They'll want to stay on their toes, as there is a constant change in ideologies that influence the overall planning processes in government.

What's Old Is New Again: Planning Trends and Influences

The phrase "what's old is new again" is especially appropriate to describe the planning trends that governments grab onto with hopes of addressing issues once and for all. These planning trends come and

go just like fast fashion. As the government is generally a late adopter, it tends to get sucked into planning trends long after they have fallen out of favour in the business world.

In *What Is Government Good At?: A Canadian Answer,* author and academic Donald J. Savoie writes: " . . . the great majority of the public sector reforms introduced in Anglo-American countries since the 1980s borrowed heavily from the private sector. They were all introduced with the promise of finally fixing government. None have lived up to the expectations. This has served to make the public sector look weaker still, when compared to the private sector. Reform in private firms succeeds or the firm suffers consequences in the marketplace." Likewise, Savoie later notes: "Various public sector reforms have made government less capable of delivering programs and services by bringing new problems and a wide array of new activities to government operations."[2]

What follows is a selection of the planning trends we've lived through. We're sharing them because like fashion, chances are they'll be rebranded and come back under a different guise.

1. Total quality management

These were the buzzwords in the late 1980s. The idea was to rally the whole organization into adopting a culture of continuous improvement, and where all employees were asked to commit to maintain high standards of work in every area of the organization. Supplier Zenger Miller was the NS government's favourite trainer at the time. It was the goal of many to attain certification and become a Zenger zealot. Once individual certification was achieved, people wore it like a badge of honour. This trend faded eventually, as they all do, but we're sure you can still find the binders, certificates and training modules in government archives.

2. Reinventing government

This was heavily influenced by the private sector and, in our opinion, failed to take into account the reality of bureaucratic structure and decision making within the government context. To do so effectively, the approach recommended government separate policy from service

delivery and, in effect, adopt a steering function and let others do the rowing. Public-private partnerships and outsourcing stemmed from this trend. The phrase that governments must move from rowing to steering became so over-used that ophthalmologists must have made a fortune treating the damage bureaucrats suffered from all the eye-rolling. Required organizational characteristics include being outcome-driven, entrepreneurial, mission-driven, customer-focused, decentralized and a change agent with the power and resources to make decisions. This approach also encouraged the use of market mechanisms and earnings as in-cost recovery.

Former NS Premier John Savage and his cabinet members were heavily influenced by this reform trend, outlined in David Osborne and Ted Gaebler's book *Reinventing Government*. Known as the "Savage years," the reform agenda included efforts to curb political patronage and stop the practice of filling certain positions with party faithfuls, as well as introducing wage restraints — all in an effort to reduce a structural deficit. This did not serve former Premier Savage well, and he and his government were affected at the next election. History was kind, however, and he is now viewed as someone who put citizen needs above partisan wishes. There are still many bureaucrats who believe Savage was fair in the way he handled budget issues related to civil servants. "Savage Days," which required all employees to take off five days without pay, were actually appreciated by many as an alternative to having a wage rollback, which was the other option being explored at the time.

Like other trends, reinventing government became passé fairly quickly, which apparently puzzled the authors. In an article reflecting on the merits of this trend, Gaebler suggested the lack of up-take was because "many public managers were simply too risk-averse."[3] It's also been suggested that the approach was a victim of bad luck and increased distrust of politicians.

3. Anticipatory government

This involves the use of forecasting, predictive data and feedback mechanisms to examine possible behaviours and events with a view to proactively managing risks and preparing for possible futures. One of us was involved in a long-term planning initiative built on this premise. A group of analysts from various NS government departments and from offices dealing with diverse segments of the population met regularly to examine population projections and assess the impact of various trends, including a shift to an older age structure, shrinking labour pool, increased urbanization and rural depopulation. The group also developed a cost projection spreadsheet to assess the impact of key cost drivers on estimated program costs. Common population projections and assumptions regarding standard drivers such as inflation were built into the tool. It was a fairly simplistic approach to projecting, meant to support planning, not budgeting. One interesting tidbit that stuck out from the work: health attributed a third of its overall growth rate to changing demographics such as aging, but projected that non-demographic factors such as physician salaries and technology would be the main drivers behind rising health-care costs — double the growth rate attributed to aging. Because this work was hypothetical, some doubted its usefulness. When a new government came to power the initiative was abandoned. This was unfortunate because the knowledge gathered was intended to help leaders make better decisions regarding the future.

4. Six Sigma

This is another practice borrowed by the private sector. It was popular in the 1990s, but only introduced to the NS bureaucracy in the mid- to late 2000s and towards the end of our direct employment with the civil service. The focus of this approach involved identifying inefficiencies, including time and financial waste within work processes. That sounds reasonable, until you realize that in many areas, government is inefficient. Consider snow removal as an example, where a certain level of service is required on provincially- or municipally-owned roads, even if only one or two vehicles are using the road in question. There are multiple examples wherein access to government services and citizens' rights to those services override efficiency. The only benefit we accrued from this trend was more work as select managers and employees went off to meetings where they could earn white, yellow, green, black and master black belts. Karate might have provided more benefits to the individuals involved.

5. Deliverology

This is described by *The Economist* as "a semi-science that takes the schemes and dreams of ministers and turns them into reality with as few disasters as possible."[4] When you think about it, delivering on your work without disasters should be a given, and one should not need a pseudo-science attached to it. Prime Minister Trudeau reportedly embraced this political planning fad that originated in the UK in 2017. Journalist Rex Murphy described a deliverologist as "… a slick confidence booster for the unprepared, for those who sweep into public office (sometimes much to their own surprise) and who promised the moon and most of the outlying planets in the hope to get there, and are now in desperate need of a hired astronomer (or consultant) to get them off the hook."[5]

Myriad Government Planning Processes and Products

The ideological underpinnings of the planning trends we've outlined above were often infused into various processes that we were expected to work through to produce a myriad of planning documents. While the trends may come and go, the planning products bureaucrats are expected to produce will likely always be around. As such, we're sharing a summary of the ones we're most familiar with.

Strategic planning

During our time in the service, strategic planning was the mother of all planning processes. There are six components to this exercise, including:

1. Analyzing the environment (internal and external) and identifying key issues;
2. Defining the mandate;
3. Creating a vision and mission statement;

4.   Identifying goals, objectives and priority areas of action;
5.   Developing a timetable to reach the goals; and
6.   Measuring and evaluating results.

While this did have value, especially in the earlier years, strategic planning exercises lost their credibility because changes in leadership, particularly political, meant we could never live up to the plans. In the end, they were more of a chore we had to endure. Quite honestly, we began to resent the time we had to put into them.

Business plans

These high-level pitches of a department's or agency's work were meant for ministerial and executive audiences and shared with the public to promote accountability. They were supposed to feed the budget development process. More often than not, the plans came after a government's agenda and departmental budgets were set. Yet, we were developing plans that, for the most part, had already been scripted and approved.

In these plans, you'd typically find an introductory message from the minister and deputy minister, followed by a departmental overview and divisional descriptions. Included was a list of key challenges departments hoped to address, followed by goals and priorities for the coming year. A section will likely be devoted to performance indicators, and yet another section containing a high-level overview of the budget and the number of full-time positions.

Despite countless hours, days and weeks of work across every department and agency, the reality was few people read these plans, and there was often a disconnect between priorities identified and resources available. We recall someone checking the number of people who downloaded a copy of a department's business plan; the count was less than the number of people involved in writing it.

Should members of the public be inclined to read these documents, they'd have to find them first. They will want to ensure a steady flow of caffeine to help them read through the jargon. They may also want to keep a pillow on the table in front of them to avoid any injuries, should they nod off.

Accountability reports

These reports are a literal accounting of what was in the business plan. They typically included summaries of work completed and charts showing how performance indicators were measuring up. Some senior bureaucrats loved to hold them up as evidence that work was completed. We saw many bureaucrats spend hours and hours filling in spreadsheets, writing documents and preparing notes to explain how departments measured up against what they promised in the business plan. These documents were funnelled throughout departments for input and review, and bureaucrats had no choice but to meet a deadline to get it back or send it along for approvals.

Understandably, governments change plans frequently and shift how resources are allocated, thereby disrupting work on various initiatives identified in a previous year's plan. Still, departments were held accountable, meaning items got carried over again and again.

We often thought a course in creative writing would come in handy when crafting content for these reports. No one ever stated they didn't achieve something; they'd shift those things into a pending category or some other nebulous hole. At times, it felt like we had more accountability to the accountability report than we did to living up to the planning commitments.

Operational plans

These plans made sense to us. The scope and timelines involved were within a department's grasp. They can help a team maintain focus on work to be done. Our advice for those developing such plans is to keep them simple, answering basic questions about what is to be done and identifying the necessary resources (financial, people and technical), timelines and individual responsibilities, so the people identified can be chased down if they don't deliver.

Action plans focused at the program or service level

These types of plans may well have had the most impact because they were context specific and relatively narrow in scope. It's easier to hone in on what has to be done, take action and then monitor to see what is and isn't working and act accordingly.

Action plans focused on an issue or area of government intervention

These exercises usually involved players from across the system, including other levels of government, and those can get messy. These plans take time, effort and, yes, paperwork, but they can result in incremental positive change. We worked on dozens over the years, including immigration, diversity, crime prevention, domestic violence, alcohol and drug reduction, tourism, economic development, waste management and self-regulation.

This work requires persistence and involves, yet again, taking one step forward and two back. We share this observation from former colleague Charlie Macdonald, who led the Disabled Person's Commission and served as senior diversity consultant with government:

> I had experienced a serious setback on a major initiative that my colleagues and I worked on for several months. After what I had considered a brilliant presentation to senior deputy ministers, one particular deputy put a pin in our balloon and the initiative was sent back to the drawing board. During my walk home, Stan Rogers's song 'The Mary Ellen Carter' came to mind and I chanted (to myself of course) the verse all the way home. Several weeks later our initiative proposal, with a few tweaks, was approved and like the Mary Ellen Carter, it 'rose again.'

Here's the verse Macdonald chanted:

> You, to whom adversity, has dealt the final blow,
> With smiling bastards lying to you, everywhere you go,

Turn to, and put out all your strength, of arm, and heart and brain, and
Like the Mary Ellen Carter rise again.

30-60-90s

This type of plan was introduced late in our careers and contained lists of items making their way to decision makers in the next 30, 60 or 90 days, including planned legislation, regulations, consultations and major communications announcements. Because bureaucrats have little control over timing, items were constantly being pushed into the next month.

Project plans

Other types of plans are also rampant in government, including project plans associated with platform commitments, as well as plans to address a plethora of recommendations arising from auditor generals' reports, expert studies and public inquiries. These were taken seriously with requirements to update progress regularly.

Reality Checks Associated with Planning in Government Environments

We were both heavily involved in the planning processes outlined, and below you'll find our take on some challenges we encountered. We hope the insights we share will help people understand why plans can go awry, as well as help the many bureaucrats and citizens who are dealing with them today.

Static mandates and a multitude of visions

First up and most difficult to change are departmental mandates, which stem from legislated responsibility. It would be rare for bureaucrats to change a mandate because, quite frankly, it's not a bureaucrat's job. Sadly, few politicians take this on; as a result, these directives tend to remain static for years, which could partially explain why the focus of government departments rarely change.

Consider provincial departments such as natural resources, environment and energy. Some think they have been co-opted by industry interests at the expense of the public good. It's now timelier than ever to have deliberate discussions and debate about these departmental mandates, given the exploitation and pilfering of natural resources and increasing threats associated with climate change. Like many things that require significant changes or shifts in thinking, governments often turn a blind eye and then seem surprised when someone points out that a department's or agency's mandate is no longer relevant to address the issues of the day.

While mandates remain relatively static, there is no shortage of vision and mission statements within government bureaucracies. These statements can be found at the departmental level, divisional level and even at individual work unit levels. Some may be inspired by a vision, but it has a deeper connection to those who had a part in defining it. Those who didn't help define the vision lack the context; it may not resonate with them, or even worse, cause them to view it with cynicism. Besides that, if a vision is not established by, or closely aligned with what the leadership wants, it runs the risk of being ignored. A vision should entice employees to line up behind their leaders in support. Sadly, we found that for many bureaucrats, there was no connection to the vision statements; they were meaningless words hanging from a plaque on a government office wall or found in a copy of a plan.

As for mission, these tended to be timeless, all-encompassing phrases that attempted to appeal to all levels within the organization. Translation: we found most were bland and faded into background noise. Over the years, we participated in efforts to define visions and missions, but we knew there could be a shift as soon as a new leader came around the corner.

Shifting contexts and environments

This brings us to challenges associated with getting a handle on the current environment. This, too, is a critical part of most planning exercises. In some planning processes, employees are expected to explore various political, economic, social, technical, natural and cultural issues from multiple perspectives. There are lots of ways to categorize the information collected, and one of the most popular is the strengths, weaknesses, opportunities and threats (SWOT) assessment. Readers who have been involved in government for a while may have let out a groan and envisioned flip charts and sharpies at the mere mention of this overused technique. Mind you, it sounds rational to undertake a SWOT analysis, but you can only apply that to the present context and environment. Planning is about what's ahead. The current context and environment can shift significantly and quickly, especially given the impact of technology. This type of analysis works in static environments, but bureaucrats — like most everyone else — don't live in an unchanging world.

Imagine the impact that COVID-19 had on government plans, or consider the election cycle, where an opportunity today could be a challenge tomorrow. For a recent example, we look to the rollback of environmental protection regulations by the Trump administration in the US. Before the rollback, these regulations would have been identified as opportunities to address climate change. With the Trump administration, the lack of regulations became a challenge for climate change policy.

When undertaking an analysis of the current environment, employees are often required to reference jurisdictional research because decision makers want to know if they are leading or following. Looking at what other jurisdictions are doing makes sense, but both politicians and bureaucrats involved in planning processes need to recognize what works well in one province or jurisdiction may not work in another due to differences in environments, population, finances and contexts.

Jurisdictional research can also be a friend or foe; it can be a challenge to persuade decision makers to take action on an issue if no other jurisdiction is doing something about it. However, if bureaucrats think the issue should be addressed, they need to work to understand a politician's, or any leader's, motives. These motives can vary from a real sense of duty to a real dose of ego. If they are driven by ego, we recommend throwing out the words "leading edge" and position them as "innovators" for being the first out of the gate.

One of us did that in our efforts to create a formal healthy workplace program for Nova Scotia civil servants. Initially, political and bureaucratic leaders were reluctant to go down the path for certification as a healthy workplace. There was talk about how the public would not understand or like spending tax dollars on civil servants, and how employers weren't responsible for their employees' health. However, they started paying attention when we presented a business case demonstrating that a program like this would benefit the bottom line and improve workplace effectiveness. We cemented approval to move forward with the plan when we pointed out that NS could be the first public sector entity in Canada to achieve such certification. This was all that was needed. It was full steam ahead. Two years later, there we were, in the Red Room at Province House, with the premier of the day accepting the certification award from the National Quality Institute's (known as Excellence Canada since 2011) CEO. Other provinces, including Alberta, BC and Ontario, followed our lead and achieved various levels of award status. Federal agencies also saw value in adopting a healthy workplace culture, with the Department of National Defence and the Canadian Forces Housing Agency following suit. Corporate organizations, including Manulife and Rogers Communication, achieved award status, as did Carleton University.

Difficulties defining and reaching goals

In the healthy workplace example, we received permission to pursue a goal. But setting goals in government is often a painful exercise because of the jargon that surrounds the process. In addition to goals, there are objectives to deal with, which are more specific than goals and have an element of measurement so they can be validated. One must also throw in some tactics for good measure, which are temporary actions needed to meet objectives for goals to be realized. Clear as mud comes to mind as we write this; you may well be thinking it's just more government *blah, blah, blah.* We admit trying to distinguish between these three different ways of capturing the steps required to accomplish anything is an exercise in wordsmithing and cutting and pasting, but bureaucrats have to do it. It undoubtedly tries your patience just reading this, so imagine the feelings of those who have to work on these plans.

Leaders and decision makers usually want employees to spell out exactly how goals will be met, even though much research surprisingly suggests complex goals are more likely to be achieved when they are pursued indirectly. British economist John Kay, who has held chairs at the University of Oxford and the London School of Economics, dubbed this idea as "obliquity,"[6] but many leaders likely won't buy into that line of thinking. For a practical example, picture rock climbing, wherein a direct route may not be the safest or surest way to arrive at your destination. Exploration and discovery may well be the better way to go. To illustrate the concept in a government context, consider government efforts to reduce crime. Many say government should focus more efforts on incarcerating the people who are committing crimes. However, setting goals linked to crime prevention through social development can bolster community well-being and be more worthwhile in the long run. This requires investments in community health and educational initiatives rather than increased investments in policing and harsher laws. These actions are more in line with public calls to defund police. Any results achieved with this latter approach would likely not be met in four-year election cycles, however; as such, long-term thinking is not readily embraced by politicians.

Another issue associated with goals involves quantity. We note that almost everyone who has worked in a formal organization has been told over the years to do more with less. Politicians are no exception to this rule, although they rarely take their own advice when it comes to setting goals. No matter how many times we tried to tell the powers that be to limit the number of goals, many seemed to think more were better.

Current research suggests an entity should have between three to five goals. Anything more than that is unrealistic in terms of achieving good results. To a great extent, we both worked in departments that attempted to stay true to this theory. Inevitably, almost every year, more "priority" goals were added to the mix, even though they were never articulated in the plans. More often than not, additional resources were not provided. Because of this, initial goals were not removed or adjusted, and no action occurred to reach them. The result was almost always the same — employees struggled to keep their heads above the water as they dealt with ever-increasing workloads and no additional resources.

This happened frequently. In one of our departments, employees held a planning session where all the departmental goals were written down on paper and taped to a wall. When tallied up, there were 39 relatively significant goals. As you can imagine, achieving these goals required lots of resources, particularly human and financial. There was no possible way they could all be achieved. Yet there we were, like hamsters on a wheel, spinning and spinning, and achieving little. We kept up our reporting, putting different items in columns indicating they were either still in progress, pending some type of approval, or occasionally even admitting that we hadn't done a thing to move something forward. Because this department was a central agency that provided services to all the other departments, what we did, or didn't do, impacted everyone else. This left us open to criticism, often justly, for not accomplishing everything that had been put forward as a priority. Many people in the department recognized we were in a no-win position year after year.

Doing our service, we found it could be demoralizing, disheartening and, at times, embarrassing to continually explain why nothing had been done on a specific goal. We, and our colleagues, wanted to show results; we wanted to feel as though we were accomplishing what was in our plans.

These practices no doubt contribute to misperceptions that bureaucrats are inept or lazy. It must also be frustrating to citizens, who are waiting for action, and upsetting to politicians, who want to publicly announce results. Bureaucrats should raise alarm bells when the numbers of goals stretch beyond what resources can accomplish.

Without fail, issues emerge. Bureaucrats are expected to free up time to address these crises. This wouldn't be a big deal if some of the goals set early in the year were taken off the plate or at least put on the back burner.

This simply didn't happen very often. We know this can be the case in any organization, but we do believe it is more prevalent in the bureaucracy because politicians have a hard time saying no, and their yeses fall to bureaucrats to complete.

Timelines to reach goals are also a challenge for a number of reasons. With uncertainty, rapidly changing external environments and four-year election cycles, bureaucrats have little or no control over timelines. Admitting this may help them keep their sanity.

Another issue affecting timelines is political expediency and the desire to show work is happening. In government circles, there is a lot of talk about identifying quick wins. We received plenty of instructions to grab the goals likened to low-hanging fruit. They were often picked first, while the rest either rotted on the tree or got put into a cellar where they never saw the light of day.

An example of a quick win could be providing a small pot of money to cover operational needs of transition houses providing shelter to victims of domestic violence, only to never engage in broader dialogue on the best ways to deliver the range of programs and services needed to address the harms. On the economic side, a grant could be issued to a struggling cultural organization that has public sympathy to keep them afloat for the short term, without further discussion on the appropriate level of financing and capacity required to support the entity in the longer term.

Inability to measure up

Yet another reality check is needed when it comes to measuring and evaluating results. Measurement became a big push more than halfway through our time in the service with pressure on leaders to demonstrate accountability. We expect many have heard the catchphrase "what gets measured gets done." But in government, "what needs to be done often can't be measured." Another catchphrase suggests "you can't manage what you don't measure." Phrases like this can make anybody's head spin.

The measurement push is leftover from the rallying cry that governments act more like businesses, where it's a lot easier to measure against the bottom line. Measurement can have value, including showing how tax dollars are spent. However, how do bureaucrats measure the value of investing billions in an education system? Or paying for seniors' bus fare on Tuesdays? The amount of time bureaucrats spend trying to demonstrate worth is the real waste. Funnily enough, we're not aware of any measurements associated with that work.

For an interesting take on measurement, we turn to *The Tyranny of Metrics*. Author Dr. Jerry Z. Muller writes:

> Accountability ought to mean being held responsible for one's actions. But by a sort of linguistic sleight of hand, accountability has come to mean demonstrating success through standardized measurement, as if only that which can be counted really counts.[7]

This sentiment rings especially true for governments and the services they provide.

In addition to difficulties associated with quantifying impacts, some measures could be counter-productive and harmful. We recall discussions with colleagues regarding measurements for prosecution services. It seemed reasonable to track the number of cases resulting in a conviction. However, should such a measure become a target, it can have negative consequences. As a society, we don't want innocent people to be found guilty, nor would we want prosecution offices feeling any pressure to pursue cases that are not in the public interest just to increase arbitrary numbers. This example shows that using certain measures can backfire.

At the individual performance level, many bureaucrats struggle at times to feel as though they have accomplished something meaningful. Correctional officers, an employee group that experiences higher stress levels than most other civil servants, have to do their job in an extremely tough and complex environment. It's difficult for them to set and quantify goals given their work, let alone demonstrate how they reached or exceeded results at year end.

Ultimately, measures reflect an individual or an organization's values and beliefs about what is important. As Andrea Jones-Rooy, professor of data science at NYU, notes in a July 2019 article: "… I consistently find that whether I'm talking to students or clients, I have to remind them that data is not a perfect representation of reality: It's a fundamentally human construct, and therefore subject to biases, limitations, and other meaningful and consequential imperfections." She further suggests, "… we've conflated data with truth. And this has dangerous implications for our ability to understand, explain, and improve the things we care about."[8]

There is an almost-absurd example: a deputy minister once asked for empirical data to prove giving civil servants a lunch break was a healthy thing to do. It was no secret that many civil servants were working through their lunch hour. In an effort to create a healthier workplace, a program was developed encouraging employees to break for at least 30 minutes. We thought we were at risk of insulting employees by suggesting the 30 minutes instead of the hour they were legally entitled to, but were advised not to "ask for too much." Employees spent three full days pulling together documentation that showed this was not just a healthy thing to do, but also in many cases, there was a legal obligation and moral imperative. It was a waste of time and energy. It was embarrassing, as a leader, to ask the team to drop what they were working on and search for the evidence to support what any reasonable person would know is a good idea. Truthfully, it was easy to find the evidence. It wasn't rocket science, though we did take some pleasure in bringing armloads of paper to the next meeting to prove our case.

We wish we could say all we had to do was provide the evidence, but even after that, deputies held a lively discussion about whether to move forward. Thankfully, good sense prevailed, and we received approval to proceed with this initiative. Ironically, while deputies were worried about public reaction, we received national attention and positive recognition for our efforts. In the end, we had something we were proud of, and other provinces looked at our efforts as we inched towards becoming a leader in workplace health.

In another situation, a new regulatory agency was set up to scrutinize the impact of any new regulations on businesses. At the time, we were working on laws to confirm the rights of people with service dogs to enter all public places. We had to run everything by the new office and when we did, we were told we had to quantify the costs — we're talking specific dollar amounts — that businesses would have to incur if they were not able to discriminate against service dogs and their handlers. Consider hotels, where some suggested room cleanup could be more time consuming. Or a taxi driver, who might have to vacuum the vehicle more frequently. A complicated spreadsheet was provided to assist with this task. For starters, people with service dogs already had those rights embedded in the *Human Rights Act*, and we were merely confirming the qualifications required to exercise this right. Unfortunately, we could not simply say "suck it up, buttercup," but we did get that result after making repeated arguments as to why the analysis was inconsequential. We never did undertake the work. The legislation proceeded regardless.

Requests for evidence of this type are frustrating to most. Valuable time and resources are spent collecting data and documentation to prove the obvious or unnecessary.

Endless to-do lists

The last challenge we want to flag is the endless list of items arising from planning initiatives that must be tracked. We should note that while some planning initiatives stemmed from political platforms, the vast majority were generated from within the bureaucracy. That's because many leaders were taskmasters and tended to micromanage those below them with demands for itemized lists of every step taken or required to complete a particular project or task. If a bureaucrat's name is attached to items in any of the planning processes we've outlined, chances are they will be required to report on their progress monthly, quarterly, semi-annually and annually. Colour-coding may be required to visually mark whether items are on track, completed, delayed or postponed. There will be inevitable delays; bureaucrats will end up spending countless hours adjusting the content again and again. It is no wonder we often thought we were acting out our own version of *Groundhog Day* because we kept reliving the process of planning, rather than working, towards accomplishing the goals.

Why Bother with Planning, Given All the Challenges?

Given the planning challenges in government, it seems reasonable to question how bureaucrats justify spending time and money on these labour-intensive activities. We posed the question to a former colleague, who served provincial governments for decades at both the departmental and central agency levels. She shared the following take with us on the merits of planning, along with advice to help bureaucrats work through the processes:

During the course of almost three decades in the system I was consistently asked by new recruits (and friends) how I could work in an environment where planning revolves around four-year election cycles. How could I put everything I have into strategic planning when time and time again a new crop of politicians arrived with new priorities, often pushing existing plans out the back door.

Simply put, I view government as a massive sandbox with lots of places to play, particularly if you have transferable skills. With the right moves, you can make several major career changes without ever changing your employer. I did and it was immensely satisfying and fast.

There were many lessons I learned along the way but I believe the ones discussed here are essential to survival.

Learn basic government 101. Understand how decisions are made, where your place is in the system and how best to support government goals.

Once you're in, you'll soon find yourself caught up in an endless wave of planning and the massive process behind it which can be soul sucking, unless you recognize the tremendous value in solid strategy. If you have good bones, they are not as easily broken. In other words, if your plan makes sense and is good for [your province, city or country], it could very well survive the next shake up. But the catch is, it must appeal to more than just you and your sense of what is right.

When your plan gets thrown to the curb (it will happen at least once in your career) know when to back down. If you have new information that will change the game, by all means make the pitch. Don't however use the same argument looking for different results. If you persist, you'll just become that 'annoying one' nobody wants to be around. Ultimately, you are paid for your advice. Give it your best. They might not take it, but at least you will sleep at night knowing you did your job.

Essentially this means never being so married to a way of doing things that you'll be crippled if it's taken away. It happens all the time, and I've personally witnessed some pretty significant meltdowns as a result. I thrive on change and learned very early in the game the true meaning of flexibility. So for me, it was an easy run.

Again, learn basic government 101. Be politically aware but not active. You need to know what they want. This means studying and understanding political platforms but in particular, those of your new bosses coming in the door. Your job after all, is to implement 'their' priorities, which by the very nature of your relationship, are now yours. You are also responsible for providing non-partisan advice. Yes, there is wording in the constitution allowing freedom of association and expression, but it might be a good idea to refrain from wearing lapel pins from the opposing team while professing your independence.

Case in Point

With planning exercises — as with most things in life — you take the good with the bad. We're going to share an example where efforts went according to plan, and another where attempts went sideways. On the bad side, one of us worked with a group of colleagues from several departments on a plan to establish a formal child death review committee. The government committed to act on the recommendation, which arose from an Ombudsman's Office report following the death of a child whose family was receiving government services. Our group spent months undertaking research, including gathering information on existing mechanisms to investigate deaths; data associated with deaths and critical injuries; as well as digging for details on various models throughout the country and further abroad. We came up with a list of models, along with their pros and cons, as well as detailed comparative information relating to the structure and the work of such committees, including the mandate, chair position, membership, reporting relationships, nature and extent of reviews, resources and public reporting requirements. We also worked on a consultation plan to seek perspectives from key stakeholders to help inform a decision. When we submitted our work to leaders seeking permission to consult, they concluded strengthening existing mechanisms would suffice, although nowhere in our documentation had we suggested that. Our group was disbanded, and our good work put on hold. It took a while for some of us to bounce back after spending so much time and effort on this important work. Fast-forward four years, where we learned that government had established such a committee.

Sometimes exercises can go according to plan and coordinate the efforts of many to do good work. Consider a provincial action plan to address domestic violence, which garnered a strong endorsement from the Nova Scotia Advisory Council on the Status of Women. The executive director said it was the first time in her 25-year career she had seen that type of coordination and commitment. It was developed with a few simple principles, which were credited for the planning exercise's success, including:

- Expanding the circle to ensure multiple perspectives were sought on what was needed and could be done with the resources available. This included getting input from those with experience, not just expertise;

- Acknowledging the good work already being done — from legislation to programming and research;
- Focusing on actions that could lead to incremental change, with timelines attached and no illusions about being transformational; and
- Deliberately avoiding the word "strategy" and instead focusing on actions, continuous learning and adaptation.

TALKING POINTS

As in previous chapters, repeat after us:

- Employees in many organizations, public and private, cannot escape planning exercises that take up significant time and energy.
- The process to develop a plan is just as important as the plan itself.
- Planning is good; but plans are rarely accomplished in the way they were initially envisioned. Don't take it personally.
- Plans can be manipulated for good and bad.
- Some old theories are the best theories.
- What is old may well be new again, so hang on to all your documents.
- Don't get attached to any one process or technique, because like fashion, trends come and go.
- Fewer goals are better.
- Failure to meet planned goals is not an option. Creative reporting takes care of that.
- Be ready to explain the obvious, even though it is infuriating.

Don't take our word for it

For some levity regarding mission statements, consider this observation made in Sarah Knight's *The Life-changing Magic of Not Giving a F*ck*. She writes: "Have you heard of the Infinite Monkey theorem? They used it on an episode of the Simpsons where Mr. Burns has a thousand monkeys typing at a thousand typewriters, the idea being that if given enough time, the monkeys could produce the works of Dickens. This is essentially how company mission statements are created, and why you need not give a f*ck about memorizing or adhering to them. They are the products of untold man-hours of "brainstorming" and "focus-grouping" resulting in the blandest, most generalized least-potentially offensive, frequently asinine copy that could have been created by any group of monkeys in any boardroom in America."[9]

Her advice: "I suggest that every time you encounter a corporate mission statement, rather than reading/absorbing it, you instead spend two minutes imagining a roomful of monkeys smoking cigars and happily click-clacking away." We honestly think that would be more useful to you.

Chapter 5

FIRST, DO NOTHING

"Civil service options to Cabinet is like a conjuring trick. Take any card. You always end up with the card the magician forced you to take."

—Sir Humphrey Appleby, *Yes Minister*

IN THIS CHAPTER:

- The Policy Development Tool Kit
- The Four Levers Governments Have to Address an Issue or Opportunity
- Nine Steps in the Policy Development and Analysis Process
- The Law-Making Process
- Barriers to Effective Policy Development and Implementation

We're now entering into the murky world of policy development and analysis, and we can attest there are a lot of vague and cloudy policy problems to address in governments across Canada.

We're not alone in thinking everything government does, or doesn't do, in response to a challenge or opportunity falls under the policy umbrella. This includes government plans and departmental positions on issues, as well as the programs and services in place to meet needs or take advantage of opportunities. Policies can be broad in scope, such as those established to address climate change or to improve access for persons with disabilities. They can also have a narrow focus, including policies concerning a particular industry sector or an issue such as long-term care for seniors. There are numerous operational policies that guide bureaucrats in administering programs and services, as well as internal policies governing everything from hiring to purchasing.

Academic definitions refer to policy as the authoritative allocation of values and, whether you like it or not, governments have that particular authority. Ideally, governments recognize the values held by members of society; analyze the possibilities for action in keeping with those values; and commit to action that, by default, becomes policy. As bureaucrats, we, like many other colleagues, were occasionally called upon to undertake the analysis and present policy options to elected leaders.

This is the policy world we explore in this chapter. We're calling this chapter "First, do nothing," because we always included this option when we presented policy choices to elected officials for consideration. Maybe you're thinking that's fitting; governments are often accused of doing nothing, or at the very least, not doing enough. While some in policy circles thought it was a cop-out to include "doing nothing" as an option, we think governments can benefit from a solid analysis on the pros and cons of not acting on some policy issues. That's because one can also argue government has extended its reach into too many areas, with resulting burdens on taxpayers and citizens.

We both became especially interested in policy when we found ourselves on unsteady ground following a decision by government to shut down an "arm's length" arts council. The decision was controversial, generating negative media coverage and anger by many who took it out on elected officials and the bureaucrats acting on government instruction. We share some information on the financial drivers that precipitated that decision in our money chapter. But for now, we want to touch on some policy issues that emerged, and for which we were unprepared to address.

The first issue related to governance. Those who opposed government's decision claimed Nova Scotia would be the only jurisdiction in Canada without an independent arm's length arts council. This was misleading. We knew there were many models governing the distribution of arts grants throughout the country but we didn't have the specifics, and so the falsehood continued to spread, and the opposition perpetuated it. For example, while British Columbia and New Brunswick had independent agencies, Alberta's Foundation for the Arts was established as a crown agency, while Ontario's was a government agency directed by a volunteer board, and Prince Edward Island's operated as a not-for-profit entity. We recall jurisdictions without independent agencies reporting they were set up that way to avoid parallel bureaucracy and duplication of costs.

Many also claimed that elected officials would be deciding which artists or organizations were deserving of funding. This instilled fears that certain art would not be acceptable to the governing elite. This was not true. Government planned to continue using peer jury review processes to distribute funding. For those unaware, jury review is common in the cultural sector, where committees made up of individuals with expertise in particular artistic disciplines assess the merits of applications and award funding accordingly. Because the government hadn't yet sorted out how the department would administer the process, we were unable to give specifics. We lost that public relations battle as well. If we were more prepared, we might have had a better chance of influencing the narrative and damming the flood of falsehoods.

Before we faced that situation, we wouldn't have thought of those issues as policy choices, but we became much more interested in lining up the policy ducks after working through that experience — which included the receipt of angry phone calls to our home, name calling and letters to editors about "heavy-handed bureaucrats."

Some think policy work is boring, but not us. It's a tough slog that required critical thinking, communication skills and the ability to influence. But it provided us with opportunities to develop relationships; gain exposure with senior leaders and politicians; and engage with stakeholders and the public.

To challenge the perceptions that policy work is dull, and to help you navigate this important work, this chapter will explore a step-by-step approach to policy development and analysis that most bureaucrats use in one form or another. We also apply the steps to a hypothetical policy issue. Knowing about these steps will be especially useful for readers interested in the policy field and for advocates, lobbyists and citizens interested in influencing the policy process. If you want something from a government, understanding the policy issues and positions behind the request can help to make your arguments stronger. We conclude the chapter with a look at barriers that can impede good policy work, as awareness of such barriers could help readers navigate the rocky terrain. It's important to note that the steps involved in a good policy development process are unlikely to vary across governments because they are entrenched in public administration studies. It's also reasonable to assume it may take longer to work through the process in the federal system, given the complexity of issues and the broad geographic scope of their policy priorities.

The Policy Development Tool Kit

Because policy development and analysis can take their toll, we envisioned keeping an imaginary policy tool kit handy at all times, just like an emergency kit in a vehicle. It provided us with comfort and eased some pain when we hit bumps along the way. The must-haves for the toolkit included:

- Rose-coloured glasses, because it was not always possible to critique a bad policy idea. These helped us be more agreeable. The glasses were also worn to help maintain a positive perspective and belief in what's possible, given inevitable barriers that came our way;
- A flashlight to shine light on the issues and help lead the way down a darkened path;
- A wrench to help us maintain a grip when curveballs were thrown our way;
- A scale to remind us that balancing competing interests is critical; and,
- A transformer, because there were expectations that we could be all things to all people.

Revisiting this tool kit from time to time provided moments of levity as we worked our way through the policy development and analysis process. If it's done right, the work will take many twists and turns.

And, despite comprehensive analysis, there will likely never be a "right" way to solve an issue government is asked to address because problems are riddled with complexity and paradoxes.

The Four Levers Governments Have to Address an Issue or Opportunity

Now onto the serious business of policy work. Before we dig into the policy development process, we think it's important for you to keep in mind that governments only have four levers at their disposal to address any issue. This handy categorization was presented to us during our public administration studies:

1. *Education and voluntary instruments*, which bureaucrats and others refer to as sermons. You may have heard the refrain, "If education worked, we wouldn't need laws," so this option is a relatively soft approach on the scale of intervention. Governments often try this first — think smoking or seat belts — but often a more heavy-handed approach is needed.

2. *Spending and other economic interventions*, also known as carrots, which includes grants or subsidies. An example would be individual tax credits for physical activity or payroll rebates for business expansion. You can add taxes or user charges to this category, although those who have to pay will not consider these carrots.

3. *Legislation and regulations*, also referred to as sticks. There are a multitude of laws and regulations in place with penalties for breaking them. Think impaired driving laws; you could also throw in public enterprise and state provision here, where motor vehicle licensing is just one example.

4. *Alternative delivery*, often labelled as downloading, which can include outsourcing operation and maintenance; devolving services to the private sector through contractual type arrangements; as well as selling state assets. This lever has been used for public infrastructure such as schools and roads, and to deliver services such as snow clearing.

Nine Steps in the Policy Development and Analysis Process

To help demonstrate how levers are chosen, we're going to walk through the steps we applied when trying to help government decide how best to address an issue or act on an opportunity.

Theory suggests there are nine steps involved in presenting a fair and thorough overview of an issue, complete with distinct and realistic options for action and an accurate assessment of the impacts.

That may not seem like many steps, but the process is not linear. We and everybody else who worked on policy moved back and forth between the steps many times over. We also know working through them can take anywhere from one day to several years. Timing depended on where the marching orders were coming from, who was driving the exercise, who was for or against the policy and the urgency behind the call to action.

In a perfect world, bureaucrats would be given ample time to complete their policy analysis. However, we don't live in a utopian state. Consider one instance where bureaucrats were tasked with preparing cyberbullying legislation in a matter of weeks that had implications for fundamental rights outlined in the Charter. The issue was deemed urgent by elected officials, who drove the exercise, and there was unanimous support from all political parties for the legislation. The work was rushed, and the courts eventually struck down the legislation that was introduced for violating fundamental principles of justice. This may not have happened, had the appropriate amount of time for analysis been given.

In another instance, a relatively straightforward request to clarify rights associated with service dogs already entrenched in Nova Scotia's *Human Rights Act* took years. A lone backbencher, a term used for members of the legislative assembly, was driving that particular exercise with no urgent call for action from the broader citizenry, and there were divergent views on how best to address the issue.

From our vantage point, these dynamics played out again and again. For the most part, economic policy issues tended to get fast tracked, while social policy issues took years to resolve. Consider the relatively quick decision to set up a multi-million-dollar transition fund for the forestry industry in the wake of the pulp mill shutdown in NS. Contrast this intervention with long-standing demands from poverty advocates fighting for increases in income assistance rates. We believe these stem, in part, from an ideological view that lauds economic spending as investment and social spending as an expense.

It is worth noting here that such dynamics appear to have taken a back seat in the government's response to the COVID-19 pandemic, with both business and personal lifelines launched rapidly. Many of the time-consuming bureaucratic processes were also bypassed for expediency, which many have hailed as a good thing — including us. We expect there will likely be lots of finger pointing later if efficiency sacrificed proper bureaucratic checks and balances.

No matter what the issue or the time assigned to the task, we and our colleagues did our best to live up to the theory and consider all the steps in the policy development and analysis process.

Let's look at the various steps by utilizing a hypothetical policy issue associated with provincial parks. Parks are a highly charged area of public policy, even when the coverage is satirical as the producers of CBC's show *This Is That* discovered when they ran a segment about government proposing to charge visitor fees based on the wildlife encountered during visits. The phone lines lit up with people aghast that any government would consider such a thing.

The policy dilemma for this exercise pits stewardship and social responsibility against finances and economics. While our example is for illustrative purposes, the sustainability of parks is an issue facing many governments today.

Step 1: Problem definition
It sounds perfectly reasonable that problem definition would be the first step in the policy analysis process; that seems simple enough. But trust us when we say the problems governments are asked to address are rarely clear. In this step, we were required to answer basic questions

about the situation, including the what, why, who, how, where and when. This was difficult because most problems in government are complex, riddled with paradoxes and conflicts, and they are inextricably linked to other issues, often overlapping or intersecting with others. Complicating this is the reality that many politicians and citizens have already defined the problem and believe they have the answer. They may only be looking for bureaucrats to find evidence to support the answer and shape it into policy. In these instances, we did our best to convince leaders there was more to the story and shared evidence to support further analysis. We tried to spend as much time as possible on this step because we knew if we could clearly articulate the problem, possible solutions would be easier to identify.

When considering the problem in our hypothetical parks example, we ask you to first imagine a government bureaucracy struggling to sustain the ecological, economic and recreational values of provincial campground park operations in the era of cutbacks. At the same time, private sector campground operators are complaining that provincial campgrounds are cutting into their revenue because government sets artificially low rates for campsites. Other commercial interests are clamouring for a piece of the pie, suggesting they could help government make revenue by offering services within campground boundaries.

It won't take you long to discover this area of government service is underfunded. Budget pressures include aging infrastructure and declining resources with little money for new developments. Staff may tell you they are concerned with protecting the system's natural and ecological integrity. At the same time, people visiting parks say they want better services. Local and municipal organizations likely also have a vested interest in this issue, given their interest in maintaining these gathering spots to serve the community.

It's reasonable to suggest a provincial park system is a quasi-public good wherein government has a protective role to play. This is especially true given the erosion of public land bases and cries from population segments on the need for more protection. There is a benefit to the public in terms of conservation and access to a limited public resource.

If the market were the only provider, there would be nothing stopping economic interests from selling off the land or making such lands into private domains. The so-called invisible hand of the market could negatively affect the sustainability of the resource through development and bypassing preservation goals. The opportunity cost could be considered too high. What would happen to all the jobs filled by civil servants working in the parks?

The private sector could argue the government is subsidizing the competition, putting them at a significant disadvantage. They could say the economics behind government owned and operated parks makes little sense, resulting in oversupply and inefficiencies, since fees are below market value and don't cover the cost of operation. Of course, selling parks to private interests could replace a government monopoly with a private one.

These competing concerns and issues usually result in divisiveness. Identifying a solution acceptable to all is difficult, if not impossible, to achieve. Often individuals or groups end up sticking their heels in and fighting to preserve their position on the issues.

At this point and with this broader context in mind, we think it's reasonable to suggest the problem in this case comes down to a lack of clarity regarding government's role in providing provincial park services, as well as the relationships governments should maintain with the private sector.

Step 2: Research and analysis

Once we had a handle on a problem, we moved onto research and analysis. This second step required homework. It included reviewing what governments were currently doing about the problem and identifying if and where other governments or organizations were taking action. Figuring out what drove the issue or opportunity was also helpful. Was it an economic issue or a social issue, or perhaps it was fiscal or regulatory? The list goes on. We found there was often more than one driver. Reviewing or initiating studies and generating statistics were also a part of this step, as was public engagement.

Hopefully, bureaucrats will be allowed to determine what the public or stakeholders think about the problem. As we noted in Chapter 3, engagement makes many politicians and senior leaders nervous because they have little control over the outcome of such exercises so there usually is some convincing required. Typical ways that bureaucrats gather feedback from the public and stakeholders include issuing discussion papers, hosting open houses or conducting polling or doing all of the above in an effort to capture the wisdom of the crowd. We also made attempts to explore links to government commitments and possible supports from across the system. This is what we referred to as the "alignment" piece, or "fit with government priorities."

With the results from Step 2 in hand, we would then revisit the problem in Step 1 because policy is an iterative process. The way we initially defined the problem often needed to be tweaked.

Using the parks example, critical activities during this step would include reviewing existing park policies and management practices, along with a review of budgets, visitor numbers and revenues. Gathering stakeholder views (both internal and external) would be a must, as would be reviewing other studies on the system and market trends (potential and demand); and undertaking a comparative analysis of policy in other jurisdictions. Besides preservation and protection mandates, it would be important to identify other priorities associated with park ownership, including tourism and economic development.

Step 3: Identify intended outcomes and evaluation criteria
During this step, we were often required to stargaze. We had to identify intended outcomes or desired results, as well as evaluation criteria associated with any proposed policy direction. This required describing what the world would look like if the problem or opportunity were addressed from afar. It also involved identifying the criteria we would use to assess which policy options would most achieve the desired results. During our years of service, standard criteria used to assess policy options included: the effectiveness of a given action; whether it was politically and administratively feasible; whether it was efficient

and cost effective; and whether it was fair or equitable.

Referring to the parks example, a goal for this step could be to ensure a sustainable park system that strikes the right balance between ecological, economic and recreational objectives. Some criteria to rate the options could be financial viability; the impact on ecological and recreational services; the impact on key stakeholders; whether an option is politically feasible; and whether the option is fair to citizens and other vested interests such as employees.

Step 4: Identify policy options

This next step is where the fun starts for policy workers. At this point, we were able to identify policy options and outline the pros and cons of each using the evaluation criteria identified in Step 3.

When identifying the options, we were often warned not to fall into the trap of listing the three typical options of status quo; what you want; and Armageddon. We've been guilty of using this tactic, which can also be described as contrasting a preferred alternative policy with a set of unrealistic ones. While working with colleagues across the country, we learned we were not alone in using this approach.

When identifying options, we tried to keep the following observations in mind, which we also gleaned from our studies:

- Don't expect a dominant or perfect policy alternative;
- Avoid settling on a favourite choice until all the alternatives have been measured against the criteria you've identified;
- Ensure that alternatives presented are mutually exclusive, and that they are consistent with available resources;
- Avoid kitchen sink alternatives; and,
- Beware the danger of falling into the over-advocacy trap, where agreement is reached too readily with vested stakeholders on the nature of the problem and the responses to it.

Back to that parks example. One option could be to keep the role of government as it is with an increase in the fees government charges people who use the parks. This would let the market decide. But beware: fees are never popular, and any changes to fee structures will probably require executive council approval. This option could be a political headache and would therefore score low on the political feasibility front. Another option could be continued public ownership of the land base and introduce new private sector partners to run certain aspects of the operation, such as concessions. Picture Tim Hortons, McDonald's or Subway setting up kiosks in the parks, if you will, but this is assuming a business case could be made. Another option could be to partner with a community organization or another level of government to run these spaces as not-for-profit enterprises. Yet another option could be privatization. The pros and cons of each option would need to be spelled out and the options assessed according to the criteria identified in Step 3.

Step 5: Consultation

We're now moving on to consultation, which is in addition to the engagement we identified as part of Step 3. This consultation is about getting feedback on specific options, and while governments are hesitant to consult, there is no good excuse to avoid sharing and receiving information given the myriad of consultation options out there.

During our years of service, this all-important step was often shortchanged due to a lack of resources or government's reluctance to consult with the public. We heard this from colleagues in other jurisdictions as well.

It's been our experience that early consultation with significant partners can help the process run smoothly. As an example, when developing a major human resources policy, the unions, whose members would be impacted, were brought into the discussions at the outset. This allowed us to get their endorsement. This, in turn, meant a lot to their membership and helped us get the much-needed buy-in to make the policy implementation effective.

We share more reflections on consultation in Chapters 3 and 9, but for now let's look at the implications of this step for the parks example.

Given the interest in parks, it's safe to say that many would want to weigh in on the options. A big challenge here would be to decide on the approach to take. Does government show all its cards upfront or ask people what they think about the role of government when it comes to running parks? There would need to be a budget to undertake the consultation. It is expensive, and as such, money will dictate the techniques, tactics and timing.

Step 6: Identify preferred options

At this stage in the process, we often had a preferred option identified for government's consideration. But the work was far from done. This was the point where the rubber hit the road as we outline in the next step. With the parks example, ideally this would be based on the evidence collected in the steps outlined above. However, bureaucrats could be directed to recommend the option most aligned with current government ideology, and the preferred recommended option could be influenced by how close government is to an election.

Step 7: Policy design, implementation and communication

There is a lot of heavy lifting in this next step. We had to list all those affected by the preferred option, including other departments, civil servants, politicians, special interest groups and citizens. We also had to share specifics on timelines and deliverables, and prepare a summary of a litany of impacts, which we grouped into standard categories such as: financial; built, including infrastructure and technology; environmental; human; social; and legal.

Years ago, the term "policy lens" became popular, with a requirement to look at proposals through a variety of lenses. These included examining intergovernmental impacts, impacts on equity groups and that ever-present "red tape" assessment. Working through these lenses took time; the impacts were not always straightforward. We also experienced situations where there was resistance because those with a vested interest in a particular option did not want the true impacts captured.

Plans to communicate the decision had to be spelled out in great detail.

Everyone who was anyone wanted to weigh in on whether the decision was considered good or bad. As we note in Chapter 9, government communications are carefully scripted to protect the governing party's image, or to boost it. Sometimes getting approval of the communications plan took longer than approval of the policy. All the bases had to be covered, with attention paid to how it would play out in the media. This is where we were expected to tap into special powers such as ESP or fortune telling; decision makers wanted us to tell them exactly how key stakeholders would react. Contingency plans were also needed to respond to stakeholders who were identified as not reacting favourably.

With respect to that parks example, everybody would want their say. If the recommendation is partnering with the private sector, you would need to be prepared for push back from within and outside a government. There would be a ton of questions. For example, how will government identify partners? What about the impact on employees? How will a government hold partners to account? The list goes on and on.

Step 8: Performance monitoring

This is where we had to outline how a government could go about evaluating whether they're meeting the outcomes identified in Step 3. These often haunted us when it came time to report on progress. We tried to be realistic on what could be done to monitor progress, because doing so required staff and resources, including capturing and analyzing data.

For the parks issue, "Show me the money" is a good mantra. Is the recommended option going to provide government with the money needed to sustain the parks? Is it going to reduce costs to the government while balancing preservation goals? What data will be collected, so a government will be able to report on progress? These are tough questions with absolutely no right answers, no matter what others will tell you.

Step 9: Approval

Finally, this is where we hoped we'd receive approval of the work. But we soon learned not to breathe a sigh of relief at the notion of this last step. Instead, we had to breathe deeply to get through the many hoops that followed. In some cases, we had to fill out a template. You can find the various forms required in Nova Scotia online — including requests for legislation or memorandums to executive council — and they can be telling regarding what decision makers want when considering policy options.[1] The Northwest Territories has an executive council submissions handbook online,[2] and we came across a link to the templates required for the Government of Canada.[3] With more digging, we expect people could find sample templates that are used in each province.

With a draft of the required documentation in hand, we had to run it by what seemed to be a cast of thousands. This cast included lawyers, accountants, communications people, and program people in the department, along with central agency employees and political staffers such as executive assistants. While they had good intentions, we found ourselves resenting what seemed like meddling from employees at central agencies and the premier's office. They constantly tried to poke holes in our good work, especially if our options or analysis did not match what they wanted.

For the parks example, you have to be prepared to work, rework and then work through the paperwork again and again. Yes, we are repeating ourselves. Trust us, you will, too. All the people in the chain of command will need to provide their two-cents worth. Unless it's the status quo, any action will be met with resistance by some and rejoiced by others.

We'll wrap up these steps with a shout-out to a guide produced by Manitoba's Auditor General's (AG's) Office on the policy development process. Although it dates back to 2003, the paper contains many words of wisdom. It was developed following a review of policy development capacity within the Manitoba government, with the AG's office identifying "a gap in terms of available guides to assist policy practitioners." It is aimed at those responsible for the policy function, as well as policy analysts.[4]

The Law-Making Process

If legislation is recommended and bureaucrats get the green light, you may have guessed by now there's a lot more to the process. Drafting instructions will have to be prepared and submitted to the office responsible for preparing bills because governments have legislative counsel bodies responsible for crafting legislation.

Preparing the instructions is usually a joint effort between departmental policy analysts and solicitors who then submit the instructions to the central legislative office. Lawyers in that office then draft the proposed legislation for government's consideration. There will likely be much back and forth before the bill is introduced in the house. In our experience, these groups have power because they wield control over interpreting policy objectives, which is translated into legal terminology. They can also slow down or speed up the rate at which legislation gets processed. Another point of interest is that bureaucrats working in this shop may be responsible for dealing directly with all parties, something most bureaucrats rarely do.

Once the bill is drafted, more paperwork is needed to get approval to introduce it into the house of assembly. Bureaucrats will be working behind the scenes to prepare the minister for introduction of the bill, including drafting briefing notes, speaking notes and Q&As.

Most legislation originates with the government where the paperwork must make its way through cabinets and the houses of assembly, or Parliament and the Senate federally, before it can receive royal assent.

Former provincial politician and author Graham Steele offers this summary of the five stages to the law-making process in Nova Scotia. The stages in the passage of a bill include:

> First reading is introduction. It's automatic and takes about
> 20 seconds. There is no vote. Second reading is 'debate in
> principle'. Every MLA can speak for up to an hour, and
> they can speak only once. Second reading can be over in
> minutes, or it can go on for days. The Law Amendments
> Committee (LAC) is a committee of nine MLAs who hear

from the public. Any member of the public can ask to appear. LAC can also consider whether to make changes (amendments) to the bill, but it doesn't have to. The Committee of the Whole House (CWH) is a clause-by-clause examination of the bill. It can take a minute, or it can take up to 20 hours.

Third reading is where any final speeches are made. The bill cannot normally be amended on third reading. Third reading is usually quite short.

With one exception, a bill comes into effect (i.e. it is the law) as soon as it passes third reading and receives Royal Assent. Sometimes the bill itself says it does not come into force until a later day, or does not come into force until proclamation. If the bill says it comes into force on proclamation, then the Cabinet decides when it will come into force. Some bills pass through the legislature and receive Royal Assent but are never proclaimed.[5]

It's worth noting here that most provincial jurisdictions refer to elected representatives as members of the legislative assembly (MLAs), although in Ontario they are called members of the provincial parliament (MPPs), while in Newfoundland they are identified as members of the house of assembly (MHAs). Quebec's elected representatives are members of the national assembly (MNAs).

We aren't aware of any major differences in the processes governments in Canada undertake to introduce and approve laws, although there may be variations in the titles of the committees that work through the stages. This includes the law amendments committee Steele references above, which he suggests should be called a public hearings committee because that is what it does. There is also one key difference between the federal and provincial governments, which is described as follows: "The federal Parliament is a bicameral legislature, meaning there are two legislative bodies: the House of Commons and the Senate. In order for federal legislation to be enacted, it must be passed by a majority in each body.

Provincial legislative branches, by contrast, are unicameral, as there is only one legislative body (referred to as the legislative assembly, national assembly, or house of assembly). These provincial legislatures operate much in the same way as the federal House of Commons. Members are elected at the local constituency level and are responsible for passing all legislation under their respective jurisdictions."[6]

For additional information on other government processes, there is a guide to "The Process of Passing a Bill" at the federal level,[7] as well as a guide on "How an Ontario Bill Becomes Law."[8]

Barriers to Effective Policy Development and Implementation

Now that we've outlined the steps, we can expand upon a few of the more significant barriers that get in the way of good policy work.

They know what they want and they want it now

According to the theory, and common sense, cabinet submissions should be impartial and evidence-based with reasonable options and clear recommendations. The risks associated with each option should be identified along with mitigation strategies. The above does not take into account the reality that decision makers sometimes want things that don't align with the evidence or there simply is no evidence. They want what they want and they wanted it yesterday. We called this decision-based evidence making. As an example, governments have bought into incentives, including payroll rebates, as a way to attract businesses. Given the number of businesses that failed to live up to their end of the bargain, we can't help but wonder how many of these requests went through a detailed assessment of the risks and benefits.

A former colleague Jim Baker, who spent more than a decade as a senior policy analyst and cabinet advisor, shared the following observation with us: "In many instances, evidence-based decision making is aspirational rather than realistic. It may be impossible or impractical to achieve because the evidence does not exist, is inaccessible or is too expensive or difficult to obtain. This doesn't mean that decision-based evidence making is the alternative, but highlights the fact that evidence-informed decision making may be the only available standard."

The desire for a quick fix

In some cases, an issue will blow up overnight, and decision makers are under pressure to act quickly. The result is limited analysis, often based on a simplistic view of any situation. Top that off with risk aversion and you've got a recipe for bad policy making. Political expediency is an impediment to good policy work. We referenced cyberbullying legislation earlier, where the fallout was significant when the legislation was passed only to later be tossed out by the courts.

Maintaining the status quo

Sometimes governments don't want to draw attention to issues and therefore they go unaddressed. This is especially true if an election is looming, as it is a time when any potential controversy is to be avoided at all costs. Social issues, in particular, are emotionally charged with no easy answers. Research could uncover issues that need to be addressed and could cause problems if government doesn't have the resources. Some examples that come to mind include long-term care for seniors and residential care for persons with disabilities. Ask anybody dealing with these service areas, and you will hear about how dire the situation is because the shortfalls in services have not been addressed. The COVID-19 pandemic finally highlighted problems with long-term care in many provinces that, until then, governments had simply avoided and minimized.

The right answer

In other instances, decision makers think they know the answer so they fail to support the research and consultation that should be undertaken before decisions are made. Elimination of the NS film tax credit comes to mind, where many felt government pulled the rug from under the industry without any consultation and no understanding of the economic fallout.

With these barriers in mind, we encourage anybody — whether working on government policy or trying to influence it — to maintain a rational, professional and impartial approach to problem solving and to continue advising leaders to do the same. As citizens, we all benefit when thoughtful steps are taken to solve problems.

Case in Point

To help readers further grasp the complexities associated with policy work, consider a dilemma that has been brewing for some time in NS, centring on aquaculture policies. As of 2020, opposition was mounting against industrial-scale open-pen salmon lots proposed by Cermaq Canada that covered large portions of NS's coastline.

The first thing that jumped out for us regarding this policy area is the inconsistency in jurisdiction over such operations, with the federal government having control on the west coast while provinces retain oversight in the east. There are also significant contradictions relating to mandates, where the federal government is phasing out open-pen salmon in BC, while Atlantic Canada appears to be courting such businesses. As noted in a CBC article, "The commitment to scrap open-net pen fish farms in British Columbia — unveiled during the fall federal election — will leave Canada with different rules for fin fish aquaculture on both coasts."[9] Ministers from the Atlantic provinces do not appear to be onside with banning open-net pens on salmon farms with the above article sharing this quote from NS's minister: "As long as the federal government allows us to keep doing what we're doing, we'll be very, very happy."

Cermaq then announced it will not proceed with a proposed expansion on the east coast but that doesn't mean similar proposals won't "align" with provincial policies. The 2019–20 business plan for Nova Scotia's Department of Fisheries and Aquaculture stated production values associated with the industry were "expected to continue to increase as the first new site applications begin review under our new regulatory framework." The plan further noted the department would "encourage new applications." With policy statements like that, we have no doubt bureaucrats will be busy working to live up to the commitments outlined in the plan.[10]

TALKING POINTS

- Policy encompasses everything governments do.
- Contrary to most people's perceptions, governments only have a few tools in their toolbox to address issues or act on opportunities.
- Policy development and analysis is hard work, but following the key steps in the process can help. If done correctly, bureaucrats will likely generate criticism along the way because no one can please everybody.
- A bureaucrat's role is to provide evidence-based advice even when the research conflicts with politicians' preconceived notions, and don't expect politicians to value that research.
- Despite what the research says, bureaucrats will sometimes be required to implement decisions that conflict with the work they have done.
- Where possible, engage key partners early in the policy development stages, as it will save time and energy trying to get them on board down the road.
- For those involved in policy development, brace yourself, because you will likely do what seems like the same thing over and over again.
- Communicating any decision will get an inordinate amount of attention as the government takes public perceptions very seriously.
- Some policies become law, which is a process in and of itself.
- Recognize that barriers to good policy work exist and for the most part learn to take them in stride.

Don't take our word for it

In a 2012 article, Aucoin notes that the decline of citizen deference and trust in political authority and a decline of partisanship in the citizenry "has meant a greater polarization along partisan lines, as parties pursue policy positions that elicit support primarily from their core supporters. Partisan polarization poses a risk to impartiality insofar as it promotes a dualistic view of politics in which those who are not allies of the government must be its enemies. This perspective sends the political signal to public servants that they need not give priority to the public service value of impartiality as the government deems impartiality a fiction."[11]

Chapter 6

GET WITH THE PROGRAM

"There are four words you have to work into a proposal for a minister to accept it. Quick. Simple. Popular. Cheap."

— Sir Humphrey Appleby, *Yes Minister*

IN THIS CHAPTER:
- The Context and Scope of Government Programs and Services
- Why Businesses Can't Run Government Programs
- Challenges Bureaucrats Face When Delivering Programs and Services
- Justifying Program Spending — Logic Models and Program Evaluation
- Drivers That Influence Costs and Demands for Programs and Services

Some people say governments don't do enough when it comes to delivering or protecting public goods while others say governments do too much. We think both statements are true and hinge on whether someone needs or uses a service; is trying to protect a public resource; or is trying to exploit a resource.

One thing is certain: most, if not all, programs and services governments deliver have a basis in legislation or policy with a stated rationale and accompanying price tag. In the following pages, we share our take on why governments run programs and include a list of various program areas. We also explore the reasons why businesses can't or won't run government programs. We look at some challenges bureaucrats face when delivering them, including the constant need to justify spending. We conclude the chapter with a summary of the drivers that influence program needs and costs.

Throughout this chapter, we use the terms programs and services interchangeably. We are focusing our insights on external programs and services delivered to individuals, communities and businesses, rather than the internal services that support bureaucracies, such as human resources, information technology and finance.

The Context and Scope of Government Programs and Services

Here's our take on why governments run programs. This is foundational, but we think it's worth repeating for context. Simply put, we live in a social welfare state with a mixed economy. That means governments play a part in the economy to ensure wealth is created and redistributed. Part of that wealth is directed to programs and services meant to improve the social well-being of all citizens, including those who cannot provide for themselves. The concept of universality was an early feature in the Canadian system, based on a belief that all people have rights to basic quality of life standards regardless of income. However, as with many things governments have provided, there has been a steady decline in universal access with many programs and services now subject to income-testing, resulting in a reduction of benefits based on a recipient's income level.

Something for everyone

We have mentioned that everyone will, at some point, tap into a government program or service because they touch on all aspects of our lives. Bureaucrats within provinces tend to focus their efforts on providing fundamental services associated with Canada's welfare state, with a huge portion of their efforts focused on health, education and social services. They are also administering programs and services associated with civil and property rights.

To provide perspective on the range and scope of provincial programming, we've attempted to corral them into categories based on broad objectives. We admit you may be tempted to gloss over this high-level categorization, but we think it's necessary to set the context, and it could be a helpful reference when you're wondering where all those tax dollars go. The list is as follows:

- Ensuring safety, including road construction and occupational health, as well as correctional services programming;
- Maintaining personal identification systems, including vital statistics;
- Ensuring compliance with policies and laws, including motor vehicle and land registration, as well as gaming and liquor control;
- Protecting natural resources, including parks and nature reserves, as well as overseeing the management of forestry, mining and fisheries on Crown land and in coastal waters;
- Stimulating economic development, including advisory services, loans and grants to businesses, as well as agricultural and aquaculture support;
- Strengthening communities, including investments in libraries, museums, sports and cultural centres, as well as programming through offices to serve diverse cultures and immigrants;
- Improving health and education through public and primary health-care services, as well as investments in educational facilities and funding for post-secondary education;
- Strengthening the social and financial well-being of individuals — from income assistance and victim services; to child protection and maintenance enforcement; from Pharmacare to home heating rebates or student loans; and from subsidized childcare and housing to placement in long-term care.

This list does not cover the full gamut of provincial program offerings. There are many more programs and services offered by the federal government, including in policy areas such as Indigenous affairs, trade, national defence, foreign affairs and criminal law. Municipal governments also offer a wide range of services in areas such as recreation, transportation, garbage collection and property development.

We would be remiss if we did not acknowledge that governments distribute grants to thousands of not-for-profit organizations that, in turn, provide programs and services to citizens in many areas, including in the social, cultural, environmental and economic sectors.

Governments also provide money to other public service entities, including police and fire departments.

You would think with all the programs on offer, governments wouldn't be in the business of creating new ones. However, elected officials love to announce new initiatives; it gives them profile, earns them votes and helps demonstrate their alleged efforts. This often translates into new or repackaged programs and services.

We witnessed much more scrutiny provincially and nationally associated with new initiatives during our last years in the service. This is a positive outcome, given the cumulative costs associated with any new initiative. Politicians and bureaucrats need to be aware that once programs are started, they are hard to stop. Someone somewhere is benefiting from every program; any program cut will be a loss for a segment of society.

Whenever we were advising on a new program, we worked especially hard to justify the need and to quantify the costs. We also tried to capture as many details as possible, including: roles and responsibilities of all the players needed to deliver the program; data needed to gauge uptake and impacts; resources required for policy, design and delivery; and capacity to support delivery, including information technology and management.

We tried to emphasize to leaders that there was little wiggle room when it came to spending. We knew many senior leaders who did the same, including Gregory Keefe, who spent close to 40 years in the NS civil service, where he occupied senior leadership roles in finance and treasury at both the provincial and municipal level. Says Keefe:

> Money is spent on a program over time as each year's
> budget allocation is made. This can give the impression
> that changing each year's budget allocation is a real option.
> The reality is that program design can, and often does,
> build in multi-year spending commitments. This is no
> different than buying a car with a five-year loan or buy-
> ing a house with a 25-year mortgage. You are committing
> yourself to spending annual amounts for years to come

and are restricting yourself for budgeting less for housing in some future year without major changes such as selling the house. Much government spending has similar long-term commitments. Even when the commitments are not as legally binding as a mortgage, the consequences for breaking them can make it seem so. Governments see it as their role to create jobs, not eliminate them, making layoffs difficult. Agencies depend on and structure themselves to deliver programs based on grant commitments. Changing those grants has immediate impact in the community. The majority of spending at the provincial level is grants, and payroll makes up a majority of the balance.

He also notes demand always outstrips supply:

I remember one decision maker getting frustrated during departmental budget presentations where department after department were extolling all the good things they could accomplish and said, 'I don't need more ideas, I need more money'. This is the central challenge to government budgets — there will always be way more need, more useful things to spend money on, than there is money to spend. Health is the primary example of this. Advances in medical science, medicines and procedures have led to treatments for illnesses that used to be fatal or life limiting and have extended life spans for people. Per capita spending in health increases with age. Each year we have more treatments to fund. I don't think there are many, if any, people that would say that healing people and extending lifetimes are a bad thing, but the implications for increasing spending is obvious.

Here, we've outlined a good overview of the range of services governments provide and reasons why there are limits to what governments can do. Services are costly and the work involved in choosing how best to meet ongoing citizen needs is not easy and shouldn't be taken lightly.

Why Businesses Can't Run Government Programs

We often heard society would be better off if we just let businesses provide the services that citizens want and need. Many also believe that businesses could do it cheaper and more effectively. Because these are enduring beliefs, it's worth repeating that the private sector, for a variety of reasons, is not necessarily a viable option when looking to provide programs and services operated by governments. These reasons include a lack of profitability and the intangible nature of long-term benefits associated with some programs, or where the fixed costs of providing services are too high. There's also the potential for corruption, overconsumption or limiting supply for public goods meant to be enjoyed by all.

As noted earlier, governments are bound by notions of universal access to essential services, as well as social and moral duties that go beyond the bottom-line mentality of the private sector. There is an ongoing need to balance competing interests and preserve the rights of citizens.

With the backdrop of COVID-19 in 2020, Nikole Hannah-Jones, Pulitzer Prize-winning reporter covering racial injustice for *The New York Times*, made this stark observation: "I never want to hear that government should be run like a business. This crisis has laid bare the dangers of gutting our public institutions and services, of depending on companies dedicated to profit rather than government mandated to work for the common good. Death is the result."[1]

Governments have also been criticized for being too big; its monopoly on some services inefficient and ineffective; and that it has extended its reach way beyond public goods to include private goods. Examples of this include alcohol, cannabis and gambling.

As a result, there's long been a rallying cry that government should be run like a business. As we noted in our planning chapter, there have been many fits and starts to apply business principles to government bureaucracies. We mentioned one of the more seminal books during our time was *Reinventing Government: How the Entrepreneurial Spirit is Transforming the Public Sector* by David Osborne and Ted Gaebler. The authors preached a focus on results, decentralization of authority, reductions in bureaucracy and the promotion of competition. They also suggested clients be redefined as *customers*. With that said, they did warn that those advocating for privatization "on ideological grounds — because they believe business is always superior to government — are selling . . . snake oil. Privatization is simply the wrong starting point for a discussion of the role of government. Services can be contracted out or turned over to the private sector. But governance cannot."[2]

When it comes to governance, elected leaders are accountable to the public, not to shareholders, and they are guided by values and principles embedded in laws that contradict being driven by profit. At the end of the day, government is a money-losing enterprise.

We lived through the push for government to be more like the private sector and found ourselves defending the nature of public service, including the need for checks and balances, as well as due diligence. These bureaucratic processes, by their nature, can lead to slower responses, which can be mislabelled as inefficiencies or ineffectiveness, but they are essential to a fair and just society.

For example, bureaucrats constantly have to ask if what is being proposed will be offered or applied to everyone or every organization with the same needs and desires. If not, the fairness principle — a key tenet associated with providing public goods — will be jeopardized. A highly emotionally charged example of this involves coverage for certain drugs for people fighting a disease. We consider ourselves lucky; we never had to provide advice on these life or death situations. But deciding to provide coverage for one person does necessitate an obligation to provide for every other citizen with similar needs. Given the cost implications, decisions like this are not made lightly. They also take time, because there is no end to the needs, demands and potential life-saving interventions that could be funded from the public purse.

In addition, some traditional business management assumptions simply don't work well in government, including notions such as "customers are always right." If that were the case, we wouldn't need laws. The label "customer" also implies people can choose suppliers, and for most government services that simply isn't the case. A government is often the only supplier of critical programs and services, and in some situations, people would prefer not to be a customer — such as when they have to pay a fine or pay a fee for service. We think it's more appropriate to refer to those dependent on government services as clients or citizens. Of course, we think it's fair to use "customers" for those purchasing goods they can get elsewhere, such as liquor and cannabis.

Another prevalent assumption is that organizational performance can be measured and evaluated objectively. On the surface, that sounds reasonable, but as we've outlined in Chapter 4, it is near impossible to measure the many intangible costs and benefits of government services. There have been lots of attempts to quantify such costs, including full-cost accounting exercises. We have participated in some of these exercises and found them inadequate and time-consuming. Sometimes they actually did more harm than good, because while it was relatively easy to capture costs of running programs and services, the benefits were more elusive; therefore, the analysis was compromised.

We also ask you to keep in mind that in business, profit is the measure of success. As you'll read in Chapter 7, for years, governments spent more than they took in. Needs are pricey and the cost of infrastructure and investment needed to run programs are often far more than the revenue generated from programs, even those with fees. One of us recalls the government trying to institute a cost recovery model — not even a profit model — for ferry operations in the province. The outcry was loud and unrelenting, so compromises were reached. The ferries continued to be heavily subsidized. People depended on these services, and the fees that would have had to be charged to cover costs would have constituted a hardship and made the service beyond the reach of those who used it. As an aside, all public transportation is highly subsidized. Too bad those working on the Yarmouth to Maine ferry service in NS didn't use that as the rationale for continued operation, instead of suggesting it could break even or make money.

Another tenet of business operation is that managers can be autonomous and accountable. This can happen in government bureaucracies to a certain extent, with many bureaucrats acting autonomously and held to account for managing their human and capital resources. However, as we outlined in Chapter 1, ministers are ultimately held to account in a democracy and that gives them the right to direct decisions on budgeting and programming, including overriding any decision made by a bureaucrat.

One last premise of business practice is this: good ideas can be acted upon immediately and bad ideas tossed aside. If only it were that simple! Political considerations and bureaucratic checks and balances make it difficult for governments to act quickly. Although bureaucrats can step up to the plate when they have to, as demonstrated with the government's rapid response to COVID-19. In the majority of cases, governments shouldn't turn on a dime; people rely on the stability of various programs and laws. Vested interests also make it difficult for governments to remove themselves from areas that may be costly and no longer serving the public well.

We hope providing this information will give you pause for thought next time someone says that businesses can do a better job running public services. Both have a role in society, but that's like comparing apples to oranges.

Challenges Bureaucrats Face When Delivering Programs and Services

We are sure that governments will always be in the business of running programs and services for a myriad of reasons, including improving well-being and quality of life for citizens. We also know that providing these programs and services are fraught with challenges for those who deliver them. Ask anybody providing services to the public, and you'll get your share of frustrations and horror stories. But bureaucrats also have unique challenges piled onto these everyday frustrations, which we explore below.

Public scrutiny

For many bureaucrats, one area that is particularly difficult to deal with is the public scrutiny that results when mistakes are made. Lots of people buy into the stereotype that government employees make more mistakes than those in the private sector, but we think that's because of the attention the media pays to them. We recall one situation, where employees involved in producing an annual NS tourism map made an error when the files were digitized. The name of a county was left off the map. The premier at the time happened to be from that county; that gave the story a lot of legs. The story dragged on, as did the claims of incompetency, with demands the employees responsible be fired. These were the same employees who faithfully delivered flawless projects for decades until this one slip-up. Thankfully, the people above them had their backs; they recognized this error was unintentional and noted that mistakes simply happen.

Former colleague Fred Honsberger, who served as the executive director of correctional services with the NS government, faced much scrutiny over the years. He wisely notes that despite best efforts and good intentions, it is not possible for those working in challenging environments that are subject to public criticism to always "get it right." Ultimately, the delivery of government services involves people working with people. He says:

> Mistakes in all organizations are inevitable, and they should be acknowledged. Unjustified criticism is also inevitable. The enigmatic nature of some government services will attract criticism based solely on hearsay, assumptions and broader political positions. Such views often represent polar opposite extremes. While constructive benefit can be derived from any form of complaint, concerns from these polar extremes are typically situation specific, lack balance and based on information that is incomplete, incorrect or biased. By implication, they attribute the perceived shortcomings of staff to lack of knowledge, lack of understanding, lack of

caring, lack of intelligence and / or indifference. This situation is discouraging for professional staff who are proud of the work that they do in a tough environment.

The face of government

Another challenge is dealing with clients who are dissatisfied with the level of government service available. Alternatively, they simply don't want to pay for the service. As we said earlier, bureaucrats are the face of government and often the only government person an individual interacts with. Therefore, it's not unusual for bureaucrats to get blamed for everything a client believes is wrong with government. This extended to our personal lives, with friends often blaming us when government did something they thought was wrong. We were expected to comment even though it had nothing to do with the roles we were in or the departments we served. This made us feel defensive, and because we didn't have the information they thought we should have had, they assumed we were uninformed. Unfortunately, that aligned perfectly with their stereotype of a civil servant. We tried not to take it personally and developed a thick skin over the years.

Mandatory participation

Law also mandates that citizens must participate in some government programs, such as motor vehicle registration. Those who have had run-ins with the law have no choice but to appear in court. It's fair to assume that most of these citizens would prefer not to use these programs. Frequently, bureaucrats delivering these unwanted services and programs had to bear the brunt of the individual's frustration or unhappiness.

Blamed for lack of choice

We've also noted earlier that many individuals don't have choices when it comes to dealing with governments. This can add a layer of frustration for them and in turn they blame bureaucrats. Government programs are highly subsidized by taxpayer dollars, and most people could not afford them if they were only offered through the private sector.

Private schools and private health care, where profit is the motive, are good examples. Other programs involve providing necessities such as income assistance, where the government is the last resort, and where the services that are provided don't fully meet citizen needs.

Securing program funding

This brings us to challenges associated with finding ways to fund government programs, which includes paying people to develop and deliver them. A strategy we used was to stay abreast of various government agendas, so we could attempt to align our initiatives with their priorities in the hopes of getting funding support. On more than one occasion, we had to scout out funding support from other departments and agencies, as well as other levels of government, to leverage additional dollars. This took time and effort, resulting in inevitable delays getting new things off the ground or expanding existing initiatives.

Entering into cost-sharing arrangements with other departments or governments comes with its own set of challenges and should not be taken lightly. As Bruce Hennebury, a former senior bureaucrat and adjunct professor with Dalhousie University, cautions:

> The feds are brilliant at eliminating funding for cost-shared programs that have created expectations and dependencies in a community, leaving provinces and municipalities holding the bag. Provinces are not innocent here either as they've done it as well. A good example in Nova Scotia is the former C@P centres designed to provide internet access to rural communities. The feds under Harper reduced funding prematurely (by community and provincial schedules) but the expectations were still there in the community, requiring the province to ante up.

The one-size-fits-all approach

Yet another challenge is government's one-size-fits-all approach to providing service. In a previous chapter, we shared details about a colleague's efforts to get the health department to acknowledge it had a duty to provide culturally appropriate health services. The "one-size-fits-all" mentality just doesn't cut it because the general public is not homogenous. This also requires being attuned to the various cultural backgrounds of citizens and understanding the historical context which influence people's lives and livelihoods. A senior leader once asked us to think about the historical context of Indigenous peoples, including colonization and residential schools, and of African-Canadians, including a history of enslavement and discrimination. The historical context of immigrants also matters, including their interactions with officials in their home country. As public servants, it was up to us to adapt — not members of the public — and while we served, we tried our best to understand needs, including participating in cultural competency training and working to engage diverse communities on their terms and through their communications channels. Near the end of our careers, we saw some evidence that policies, programs and services were more inclusive, but we know much more work is needed to meet the needs of a diverse citizenry.

Inability to meet all needs

Meeting client needs has always been a big stumbling block. And in some cases, it can cause bureaucrats great distress. At times, a bureaucrat's professional training will rub up against the reality that government programs on offer are not enough to fully meet client needs. For example, a social worker can determine what is the best level of service that a client needs for their optimal social and financial well-being. This thinking is embedded in codes of conduct governing the profession. Unfortunately, government programs are designed to meet minimum standards, and in some cases, bureaucrats have to deny service because of finances or program eligibility restrictions. We knew many bureaucrats who struggled to reconcile these conflicting values. In some cases, they were not able to build resilience and had to change jobs or quit entirely for reasons regarding personal health and well-being.

Justifying Program Spending — Logic Models and Program Evaluation

Unfortunately, as should be clear by now, there is never enough money available to meet program and service needs citizens expect from governments. Because of this, many bureaucrats spend an inordinate amount of time justifying the need for their particular programs or services. This is especially prevalent leading up to annual budget setting and when new governments are elected. Some politicians also exploit programs when nearing election times — either to disparage them or to boast about them in an effort to score political points. We often had to be ready to justify an existing program if it was a target for cuts, or we had to be ready to launch a new program that politicians promised to deliver. We made it a point to hang onto any evidence we had accumulated over the years about the worth of the programs we were involved with. This allowed us ready access to the information we needed when asked to demonstrate proof of a program's worth.

The illogical logic model

One way to capture how a program was working, and therefore deserved to be funded, was to depict it in a logic model. This is a simplistic tool governments introduced to scope out the activities and impacts of programs. During our last years in government, logic models were all the rage. Upper management insisted staff logically link what they were doing with a specific outcome associated with that work.

Logic models have their place and can be useful for simple systems when there are clear linkages between cause and effect. However, we jokingly referred to them as illogical logic models because these models assume a rational, mechanistic and static environment and rarely take into account the dispositional nature of human systems, which is government's domain.

Program evaluation

Evaluation is another area that became somewhat of a fixation with senior leaders. Such processes are another way to generate proof that a program or service is working as intended or not working as the case may be. We think this is a positive trend, but it can be taken too far.

Anybody can benefit from knowing about the types of evaluation out there. If you're a bureaucrat, you may have to carry one out. If you count on a government program, it may be helpful to know the types of evaluation the program may face.[3] They include:

- Formative, which is designed to test strengths and weaknesses during the development stage;
- Process, which assesses the implementation of a program;
- Economic, which assesses the cost-effectiveness of a program;
- Outcome, which is used to gather descriptive information about the short and medium-term results of the program, including knowledge, behaviour and attitude change; and,
- Impact, which is the most comprehensive and focuses on documenting the long-term effects of the program.

Each one of these evaluations have challenges, including the costs to undertake them and the employee effort required.

Outcome evaluations are especially challenging because it is difficult to prove cause and effect. As we've noted a few times, it's difficult to measure the intangible nature of government programs, and there are limits to the tools available. However, choosing not to measure is not an option; bureaucrats need evidence to show what they're doing is worth the cost.

Drivers That Influence Costs and Demands for Programs and Services

We're going to wrap up this chapter on programming with a look at the range of drivers that influence the costs and demands of government services. The drivers were identified by bureaucrats from across the NS government as part of a long-term planning initiative with which one of us was involved. These drivers apply to any jurisdiction. We hope knowing about these will help one appreciate why the costs of government programs and services go nowhere but up.

Natural events and the environment

This category included climate (specifically, weather); pandemics; health of natural resources; natural resource extraction opportunities; geography; and remediation requirements. Consider how much a pandemic affects both spending and revenues. On the weather front, a bad winter could throw a transportation budget out the window; a hurricane can result in the need for new programs to help municipalities and citizens deal with the fallout. On the remediation front, consider the ballooning costs associated with abandoned oil and gas wells in western Canada and the implications that will have on public finances. In April 2020, the federal government announced a $1.7 billion dollar program to help provinces clean up these sites.

Capital, infrastructure and operating costs

In this section, we included: energy use; materials; infrastructure (capacity); maintenance (fleet, buildings, equipment); technology; transportation costs; leasing costs; and postal costs.

Demographics

Here we considered: age, size, health status and diversity of the population; education and employment levels; labour market participation and availability; and employee turnover. Age alone has significant implications for health and educational programming needs. Labour market participation, or lack thereof, can also directly affect the need for programs such as income assistance as well as the province's ability to pay through the collection of income taxes.

Social demands and trends

Under this category, we looked at: expectations; policy decisions; legislation; public interest; consumer confidence/preferences; and geopolitical issues. Many laws and policy decisions have strings dictating specific programs and services governments must provide. On the geopolitical front, consider the impact on programs and services required to meet the needs of immigrants.

Financial realities

In this last category, we included energy prices and volatility; interest and exchange rates; revenue recovery; tangible capital assets; and income levels. Again, we expect everyone can relate to these because they also influence our own personal budgets and spending capacity. At a macro level, economic outlooks, the Consumer Price Index, and the Gross Domestic Product all influence revenue available to fund programs and services, as does contributions from other levels of government, including federal and municipal.

We recognize there are a lot of items in that list and each of them could be a chapter in their own right. We suggest revisiting this list from time to time to appreciate how many factors drive the demand for government services and the costs to provide them.

We hope the information we've shared in this chapter gives you greater appreciation of the value and scope of government programs and services and the unique challenges faced when delivering them, including high costs. We also hope we've challenged the perception that businesses could or should provide such services.

Case in Point

For this case study, we're going to share an instance where government did manage to stop a program. We'll let you decide if it was a good call. It involved the Nova Scotia Health Authority's decision to discontinue providing universal prenatal instruction online and instead directed parents to a list of links to other online resources. Apparently, money saved — the tool was provided under a contract with Ontario — would be redirected to other resources.

When the online tool was launched in 2014, the government claimed new and expectant parents were looking for credible information online and the content available was customized to meet NS standards. It was also free for all expectant mothers and their partners living in the province.

Fast forward a few years later. Low usage numbers associated with the online training were used to justify the decision to discontinue it, with the CBC reporting, "of the 1,229 users who registered for Welcome to

Parenting in its second year, 90 per cent didn't click on a single lesson."[4]

On the surface, it seems straightforward. There was little uptake, so why not discontinue the online training? As former bureaucrats, we know there is always more to the story. We sought out a public servant who worked in the area of prenatal care for decades. She said that cut was the last in a series of blows that dismantled government provision of universal prenatal care instruction in NS. Years earlier, the health authority in partnership with the department of health offered classes to new parents at the hospital. She said those were discontinued because the stats showed the people who attended could get the information elsewhere or pay for it. The resources spent on face-to-face training in a hospital setting could be redirected to those most in need, including location-specific options. As a consolation, online training from Ontario was adapted for use in NS, but the material was overwhelming and the site difficult to navigate. The result was a bare minimum of service, with parents directed to other online resources that may meet some people's needs, but those sources may not have been vetted nor customized for the NS context and some may come with a price.

In another CBC article on the issue, a parent notes, "I just felt it was extremely hypocritical because they made an online course that was not useful and then it was almost like they were blaming the … parents for not using it." Another parent said, "There was so much information — all of it valuable, you know, I'm not denying that it wasn't valuable — but it was like information overload." When the website was scrapped, she "felt … a complete loss of support. Having to be forced into the online courses if I wanted to learn anything, [then] to hear that those are gone as well and that there is no kind of official classes anymore, I think it's terrible."[5]

The head of Doctors Nova Scotia raised a great question about this service: "I think we have to still look at the question: how do we meet the needs of those who need prenatal education the most but still meet the needs of those who want it? And so that's going to be a larger question for the system," said Dr. Tim Holland.[6]

We think it's a good question for everyone; it touches on the role of government and principles associated with the provision of public goods.

TALKING POINTS

- Everyone at some point in time will use a government service or program.
- Government programs and services are critical to the health and well-being of citizens and to the country as a whole.
- While business practices have their place, they often don't apply to the business of government.
- Government programs rarely make a profit, and people who use government services rarely have a choice.
- Resilience can be a bureaucrat's best friend when it comes to serving the public because they all face many challenges along the way to serving the public good.
- Stepping back and assessing how programs and services are working is a good thing, but efforts should be made to keep evaluation plans and methods simple.
- There are many external factors that influence the cost and demands of government services, and for the most part, demands for government services exceed the resources available.

Don't take our word for it

In an article for the Centre for Public Impact, public policy analyst Christian Bason says, "Treating citizens as consumers reduces the relationship between citizens and government to a transactional one as if we are simply customers in a bank or supermarket. But government is so much more than that."

He suggests consumer logic undermines the purpose of government. "It's quite a dangerous place to go because it assumes we are paying as customers for an individual service. But the premise of government is the opposite. Government exists to provide goods and services with outcomes that are greater and more significant than the individual transactions and individual needs."

> If we had always taken this view of citizens as customers then we would never have created a post office or telecommunications system. These are systems that rely on the idea that some people receive services that are extremely costly to deliver (for example to those living in rural areas) whereas others receive them cheaply, but everyone still pays the same.[7]

Chapter 7

SHOW ME THE MONEY

*"We want all responsibilities, so long as they mean extra staff
and bigger budgets. It is the breadth of our responsibilities that
makes us important — makes you important, Minister."*

— Sir Humphrey Appleby, *Yes Minister*

IN THIS CHAPTER:
- Financial Underpinnings
- Where the Money Comes From
- It's All about the Budget
- Trends in Government Financial Management

We've all heard the rallying cry that money makes the world go around, and although gravitational pull is responsible for the world turning, this refrain aptly applies to governments and their bureaucracies. Collecting and redistributing money is a huge piece of government operations and without that work, every citizen would feel the impact and those most vulnerable would suffer.

Because money plays a leading role in the bureaucracy — we're talking hundreds of billions of dollars — we're dedicating this chapter to the world of government finance. We'll start with a high-level overview of governments' financial underpinnings, including the safeguards in place to manage the public purse. We'll also walk through the budgeting process, which is always contentious. We'll conclude with a look at some trends we've lived through as government struggled to rein in spending.

Before we dig into the heavy stuff, we want to tell you about a game we played with our friends who don't work for government, where we asked them to estimate Nova Scotia's provincial budget. These friends are educated, interested in current affairs and were so far off the mark, many were embarrassed. Their guesses ranged from $200 million to $1 billion and were nowhere near the $11 billion spent in Nova Scotia annually at the time of writing. And of course, the larger the province, the bigger the budget. In Ontario, the budget was estimated at over $160 billion; while in BC spending was in the $60 billion range.

We share this because we were surprised at how many had no idea of the relative size of their provincial budget. Without that knowledge, they would be hard-pressed to appreciate just how much government services cost and the work involved in managing that amount of spending.

If our friends' lack of knowledge is a barometer, we expect many people have no idea about the size and scope of government budgets. This could be why some think governments play loosely with the revenues collected and choose to spend carelessly. We've heard our share of complaints, innuendos and criticisms from the public, politicians, lobbyists, advocates, and, yes, at times even our colleagues, about how money is allocated and spent. We hope to address those criticisms by sharing information on the checks and balances that are in place and the work that goes into managing public finances.

Financial Underpinnings

We'll start the discussion with a look at the financial underpinnings that form the basis of how governments at all levels collect and spend money and how they are held to account for that spending. This includes legislative acts governing finances, which outline safeguards and guideposts.

Keepers and protectors of the purse

One such safeguard is a separation between those responsible for getting the money through economic and tax policy (finance) and those responsible for protecting it (treasury). We most often dealt with folks in treasury, who we thought of as general managers, gatekeepers and guardians of the purse. To get a sense of the relationship between bureaucrats and these financial head honchos, consider the relationship you have with your bank. It's not always sunshine and daisies. You may appreciate the protection they offer and all the administrative work they do to track your spending and investments, but they're also the first to rein in your spending when they see it getting out of hand. While this can understandably cause friction, we listened to and respected their expertise. Some would tell you that we also challenged them if we thought the spending was warranted and justifiable.

Releasing the numbers

Another check on government spending is the requirement that financial statements be released annually. Despite perceptions of wasteful spending and mismanagement in all governments, releasing this information will help to catch anything that goes off the rails for nefarious reasons, including stopping someone with ill intent or catching up with them down the road.

These public accounts of spending compare a government's financial results with the budget plan for the year. We know they are complicated and overwhelming to most, given the extent of the financial transactions made by governments on a yearly basis. We're not implying that governments purposely make these difficult to understand, but finance is a complicated area of government activity. There are hundreds and hundreds of pages to pour through. Be aware that the communications accompanying the release of such reports always try to paint a rosy picture, which many find disingenuous.

Called to account

Federal and provincial government spending is also subject to challenge by the opposition. These challenges take place annually in legislations and parliament following the tabling of a budget. In Nova Scotia and elsewhere, they are referred to as "the estimates," which is the tabling of spending plans across departments, agencies and crown corporations for the fiscal year. House rules allow opposition a set amount of time to challenge ministers on their departmental spending. Some bureaucrats are especially tuned to the timing of these sessions because ministers rely on them to explain the details behind the numbers.

Again, in NS and elsewhere, bureaucrats are not allowed to respond directly to questions raised in the house during the estimates process, which can make for some awkward moments. We sat through these processes and were among the many civil servants who jumped up out of their chair and dashed to the front of the room to whisper the answer to a question in a minister's ear at which point they would repeat out loud the words just whispered. We recall one year when a minister, who was not known for her tact or diplomacy, turned to one of us and demanded loudly enough for all in the room to hear, "You had better have a good answer." It put unnecessary pressure on us, and of course it made the minister looked ill-informed.

Coupled with the circumstance of not having a voice in this process, many bureaucrats have to deal with the sinking feeling that comes with trying to defend a minister who is being set up by a masterful opponent. In one instance, an opposition member, having done just that, gleefully approached one of us after a session, rubbed his hands together and whispered: "It smells like burned toast in there to me." He was satisfied because he made the minister look foolish. We could see it coming, but the minister was like putty in this person's hands, and she could not see it until he gave her enough rope to hang herself. Even though the opposition set her up, it was the bureaucrats who bore the brunt of her embarrassment.

Of course, ministers also use the estimates process to their advantage, including structuring their responses so they can eat up as much time as possible. They do this because the opposition is only given so many hours to grill ministers about the spending. While serving in a communications role, one of us was asked to draft an hour-long speech for the minister to deliver. Opposition members literally rolled their eyes and yawned, as they knew exactly what we were up to. During that estimates process, departments were appearing alphabetically, and in this case, there was a desire to use as much time as possible with hopes of preventing the opposition from reaching the time slot for the premier's office which came later in the alphabet.

Additional checks and balances include public accounts committees, where elected representatives from all parties get to publicly challenge government officials on spending. These committees are the only place where politicians can question bureaucrats directly, who are then compelled to respond. Unfortunately, these committees are often used by the opposition members — much like other legislative committees — to embarrass or criticize the manner in which the governing party has managed a program, policy or area of spending. We can't recall a time when an opposition party praised those being questioned.

We can assure you this was the reason why many bureaucrats experienced a sinking feeling in their gut when they realized they had to appear before this committee. Hours and hours of work go into the preparation for these appearances. Operational staff prepare briefing books, speaking points and a multitude of documents to help those appearing get ready. Senior leaders brief deputy ministers who in turn, brief their ministers. All of those attending spend time thinking about what angle the opposition will take on an issue and then prepare and practise appropriate responses.

This is another example of how bureaucrats get caught in the crossfire of the governing party and opposition who are all trying to score political points. Sadly, similar situations happen to bureaucrats across the country.

Other oversight mechanisms

Formal auditing functions provide yet another check on government finances, where, in every jurisdiction, an independent auditor general is responsible for scrutinizing spending and issuing public reports with recommendations.

These oversight mechanisms gave the opposition an opportunity to criticize a department, politician or bureaucrat for work they view as wrong, unethical, illegal or just scandalous. It's been our experience that opposition members will make mountains out of molehills, often over-exaggerating or misrepresenting spending that is, in the scheme of things, minor. Some cases have merit, but many became shaming exercises directed at all bureaucrats and politicians — a classic example of a few bad apples spoiling the bunch. Some of you may recall a scandal that erupted when a federal minister purchased an expensive glass of orange juice at a pricey hotel. Weeks were spent criticizing this action. The cost to taxpayers of attacking and defending this spending was far more than the money spent on the orange juice. Travel expenses are an easy target that instills the perception of waste in government, even though most bureaucrats are compelled by policy to look for the most inexpensive method of travelling. These distractions often take away from the discussions that should be happening about real issues such as programs that are no longer relevant or only in place to serve a political interest.

A relatively recent development on the accountability front at the federal level is the Parliamentary Budget Office (PBO) decision to cost out election platforms for parties seeking a neutral estimate of the cost of their policies. Having an objective analysis of what political promises will cost taxpayers should make for more informed voting decisions. Our former colleague Bruce Hennebury, who worked in both finance and treasury, points out that "the PBO was introduced by Harper after the sponsorship scandal as part of a host of accountability reforms, some good, some bad with unintended consequences (classic red tape which is ironic). It could play a more significant role in budget forecasting, reducing 'gaming' by both bureaucrats and politicians."

We hope our overview of the various checks and balances in place to protect public financing gives you some comfort and confidence that, for the most part, governments account for how money is spent.

Where the Money Comes From

We think it's fair to view public money as "ours" because most of us contribute to public sector budgets by paying personal, corporate and sales taxes. And of course, there are property, deed transfer and business occupancy taxes, to name just a few of the taxation measures in place to shore up the public purse. We also pay lots of fees for services and programs that governments deliver — too many, according to most people. Money also pours in from lottery and casino profits, alongside taxes associated with tobacco, liquor and cannabis.

Tariffs, royalties and federal transfers also provide revenue. Governments also collect money from fines, with plenty of laws in place where non-compliance results in the offending party paying a penalty by way of more fines. Some are fairly common and relatively inexpensive, such as parking tickets. But other fines involve huge amounts of money. Think of a company fined for breaking safety rules resulting in the death of an employee. There are even fines, labelled as late penalties, associated with tax collection. It is important to keep in mind, however, that there is a cost to governments when collecting these fines; as such, the overall amount going into the coffers is smaller than most believe.

Admittedly, it appears there is a lot of money to go around. Despite deep pockets, governments spend more than they take in and have done so for generations, hence the ballooning debts plaguing governments everywhere. This brings us to the subject of debts and deficits. To be clear about the difference, debt is the cumulative amount owing over many years and deficits are incurred when expenses exceed revenues in any given year. During our years of service, governments mostly racked up deficits, but surpluses were on the rise in the last few years. Unfortunately, at the time of our writing, COVID-19 put a strain on budgets. Many governments were falling back in the red. Consider the latest deficit projection from the federal government as of mid-2020, which is estimated at $343 billion. Even with surpluses, the cumulative debt can continue to grow because accounting rules require capital purchases and long-term lease obligations to be applied directly to ongoing debt.

One last point on spending: while governments fund many areas of activity, it's worth noting that health spending and debt repayment take up about half of the provincial budget in Nova Scotia. Health spending is about 40 per cent, and another chunk (about 8 per cent) goes towards debt servicing costs, mostly paying interest. Other jurisdictions spend a similar percentage of their budgets on health, including Ontario and BC, which were hovering between 41 per cent and 43 per cent, respectively. That leaves a little over half of the budget remaining to cover all the other services provincial governments provide, including education and transportation, to name two of the bigger spenders.

While there is no shortage of need, there are of course limits to taxation, since many believe we are overtaxed now. Our former colleague Gregory Keefe said that's a values argument. He stated: "When working on budgets at HRM [Halifax Regional Municipality] and hearing the 'too much tax' argument I was amused by the fact the cable/phone bill for the average homeowner was higher than their property tax bill. Aside from the perception of high taxes, real or not, the ability of the community to pay, competitiveness for economic development, and the mobility of capital and skills that earn high income do place limits on the amount of revenue that can be raised."

It's All about the Budget

As you can no doubt appreciate, governments everywhere make hundreds of thousands of financial transactions over the course of a year, but the one thing that gets the most attention is the annual budget. This is true for those both inside and outside the bureaucracy. In part, it is because budgets have to be tabled annually — based on a fiscal rather than a calendar year — resulting in a lot of hoopla surrounding this process.

All governments like to highlight budgets. It's where they get to brag about how they are better managers than their opposition and therefore worthy of retaining power. This is particularly true at the federal and provincial levels due to the partisan environment. While budgets provide an opportunity for parties to defend virtues associated with fiscal restraint or financial accountability, they also provide ample opportunities for opposition to poke holes and draw attention to shortfalls or spending patterns they don't like. Federal and provincial governments can fall on a budget vote; ultimately, there is a lot at stake.

Governments do not develop budgets solely to keep track of where and how money is spent. They are also developed with a few key goals in mind, including promoting economic growth; improving the allocation of resources; addressing the gap between those who have and those who don't; addressing issues associated with taxes and subsidies to achieve a specific purpose; managing public entities; and achieving goals stated in election platforms or throne speeches.

You may be rolling your eyes or questioning government's commitment to these goals given the criticisms that arise once a budget is tabled, including accusations of big breaks for businesses on the backs of the poor, as well as spending in support of political or partisan interests. Examples many people point to are the incentives to business, including loans, or the capital spending on roads and schools. We recall a few years back, where in NS, many questioned how a new school in the education minister's riding jumped the queue when documents showed bureaucrats had said there was "no benefit demonstrated" for the school. Even NS's auditor general questioned the decision-making process. Such situations do occur, but probably not as often as people think.

Building the budget

Now to some of the key elements that go into building a budget. In most cases, many bureaucrats are involved in the budgeting process. It is generally led by a corporate finance department with input from departments, agencies and citizens.

Departments are asked, generally in late autumn, to start the annual budget process. They are often given one or more scenarios to work with when developing required documents. Those scenarios may be to develop it with an increase or a decrease in budget or with no change at all in the dollar amount received. Once the departments have submitted their budget requests to corporate financial bodies, it becomes a waiting game until the budget is tabled in the house.

It is at this point that departments pick their priorities and try to secure funding to maintain programs and services, as well as fund new ones. In worst-case scenarios, departments have to determine what will be cut if a reduction in budget is anticipated. This takes a huge chunk of management time, as it should, given all that is at stake.

People may not necessarily think about emotions when building a budget, but this process highlights many difficult feelings for senior management teams grappling with budget implications. For example, tension can arise when colleagues are forced to compete against each other if they are vying for money for their particular area of responsibility. There is also the heavy emotions of worry, angst and sadness if cuts are anticipated. These cuts often lead to staff layoffs and have negative implications for clients.

Keefe said, at one level, "robbing Peter to pay Paul is what government budgeting should be all about — setting spending priorities to support program priorities and reduce spending on lower priority program areas. In reality though, doing this directly is divisive. Logically, it might make sense to say that with an aging population we need less funds for education and childcare (less kids) and more for health (seniors are more frequent users of the health system); emotionally and politically it is not practical and highly divisive. Such trade-offs need to be less direct and longer term — e.g. allow the health budget to grow while holding education flat therefore demonstrating a priority without emphasizing a non-priority."

Most often, citizens are given an opportunity to provide input into the budget process through obligatory town halls. We recall many of these road shows were viewed with skepticism, because most participants believed decisions had already been made, and officials were just ticking off a commitment to consult. Chances are a finance minister would hit the speaking engagement circuit to set the tone — whether that's spending or reining in — including appearing before chambers of commerce, given their clout in the political arena.

Another key element in budget deliberations are the assumptions built into the estimates for revenues and expenditures. A former NS finance minister told us that shortly after becoming a minister, employees asked him how much he wanted the deficit to be. This floored him (and us) until he (and we) understood there is some play when it comes to projecting revenue and to forecasting spending. Conference boards and other monetary institutions project economic growth based on the total economic activity and interest rate direction. There is enough leeway in these projections to present more or less revenue and spending depending on a government's fiscal agenda. Our former colleague Hennebury tells us that, in NS at least, there is less play in revenue forecasting than one may think, thanks to the auditor general's (AG) review of the revenue estimates. This is not to say there was none, with Hennebury adding, "I lived through the early 1990s at finance where revenue targets were consistently missed because of this 'play'. Since the advent of the AG's review of the revenue estimates in the mid 1990s, these forecasts have become more professional and generally more accurate."

Tabling in the house

With departmental, stakeholder and citizen input in hand, government decision makers will set the budget and prepare to introduce it in the house on what many call "budget day." Many bureaucrats at the centre of governments will be consumed with work during this time to prepare the necessary documents. Other colleagues will be preparing for the aftermath, including producing materials for deputy ministers to send out to staff and stakeholders. Be assured that the budget will be positioned as good news regardless of whether there were cuts or hikes in a department's budget.

There is also a lot of fanfare around budget day. Finance employees, journalists, key stakeholders, union leaders and others are literally locked in a room where they are given the first copies of the budget to review. This is done as a courtesy; this way, they have time to digest what it means before they are asked to comment publicly on their way out of the room.

We've been in lock-ups. The tensions can be palpable. Even though efforts are made to prepare various stakeholders, groups and communities that may face negative impacts arising from the budget, hearing about cuts is difficult to say the least. Over the years, many bureaucrats in Nova Scotia found out their jobs were in danger as the budget was read in the legislature. We expect this happens elsewhere.

Deception can also rear its ugly head when budgets are tabled. We witnessed an occurrence where money was taken from one of our departments — the Public Service Commission (PSC) — and given to the Department of Health and Wellness with the understanding that the PSC would retain complete control and access to that pot of money. On the books, it looked like the government was living up to an election commitment to invest more money in health and wellness initiatives.

As bureaucrats who had to live with this sleight of hand, there was a price to pay. Those in the PSC who were delivering programs no longer identified in the budget felt as though their work was not significant because it didn't warrant a budget line. Many also didn't appreciate having to play a role in the farce, which conflicted with values of honesty and transparency. The relationship between the leaders of the teams in both departments became strained. Publicly, it looked as though government kept a promise, but of course they had not.

Dealing with the internal fallout

There are other fallouts for bureaucrats once the budget is tabled and passed, especially if there has been a delay in approval. We have been in situations where the budget had not been approved until the fall, long after the start of the fiscal year in April. The reality is that bureaucrats don't sit there twiddling their thumbs, waiting for the final okay. They've gone about their business, as legislation in NS lets them spend up to 50 per cent of the previous year's budget. After, however, they could face two possible challenges. In the first instance, funding may have been cut for a project they just spent five months working on. Or, in the second instance, they may now have five months to develop and implement a new project announced as part of the budget that was not anticipated. Of course, the new project was likely built on the assumption bureaucrats would have 12 months to accomplish the stated goals, only to be left with less than half of that time.

As you can appreciate, the preparation, tabling and management of a government budget is a huge piece of work involving countless people. It undoubtedly has far-reaching implications for stakeholders and citizens.

Trends in Government Financial Management

With that overview of the budget out of the way, we're now going to explore some broader trends in financial management. Just like other business processes, there are patterns in the ways that governments manage finances. Most centre on either obtaining more money or cutting spending. Some of these apply to the private sector as well. Here are a few we lived through.

The four-year cycle (or: cut, cut, coast, spend)

In our experience, year one and two in a new government's mandate can be rough for them and for the bureaucracy. Once elected, ministers get a crash course in how little money is available, and they'll look to bureaucrats to address shortfalls. These are the years that bureaucrats are often tasked with providing evidence that their programs are valuable; that they can be delivered as effectively as the private sector; or that their budgets are not padded enough to cover trivial expenses. By year three, there will likely be some stabilization, and then all hell usually breaks out in year four when governments start saying yes to everything because an election is looming. Hennebury called this the "cut-cut-coast-spend" four-year cycle of a newly elected majority government. In that spending phase, they may be especially open to providing grants and subsides to businesses and organizations so they can plan photo opportunities. Bureaucrats are often ready with their wish lists, too, because politicians may ask for investment opportunities.

The spending cycle noted above was captured in a graph presented to us by one of our Dalhousie University class professors. The graph tracked government spending over the years, where there was a distinct pattern of ups and downs in four-year cycles. At the time, the only exception was the "Savage" years we mentioned in an earlier chapter where spending in NS remained flat. That government paid a hefty price with dismal results at the polls after their first mandate. In a *Chronicle Herald* article on "The Savage revolution," a former minister said that cabinet was "prepared to decide matters in the provincial interest and (to) place political considerations second."[1] Sadly, in our opinion, this attitude is an anomaly, but if all parties had that attitude, it would benefit the citizens, and ultimately, the governing party in the long run.

Death by a thousand cuts

Another distinct pattern in financial management is the constant need to look for ways to reduce spending because most departments have been facing cuts for years, even when governments have surpluses. Even in the scenario where the department may be allocated the same budget as a previous year, there is still less to go around because of salary increases and increased costs to operate programs. In effect, the budget process while we served became a cost-cutting exercise.

When a government is in a cutting cycle, there are only three methods available. First is pure economics, which has been described as a game of chicken wherein governments can stop doing things or sell assets, and decisions are usually based on how loud people will voice concerns. Abandonment of lighthouses is one example at the federal level, where government walked away from the responsibility of maintaining many of these historical assets located across the country. Secondly, there is the economics of trimming, which tends to be more "sellable" to the general public. Here, the focus is on spending freezes, especially salaries, and those elusive efficiencies. The third and final option is the economics of delay, for which governments are notorious. Consider the state of infrastructure as an example where upgrades are held off as long as possible. We believe this cost more in the long run than if governments had invested regularly to keep the infrastructure in good shape.

Despite best efforts to apply the first method and show how governments can save big money on unnecessary programs (as in former partisan investments), those above will probably go for the second method. Political science professor Donald J. Savoie backs up this claim in *Whatever Happened to the Music Teacher? How Government Decides and Why*. He writes: "My own experience as an adviser to various governments at both the provincial and federal levels, as well as abroad, suggests a pattern: politicians want to squeeze savings from government operations and bureaucracy; but public servants insist that if significant savings are to be realized, the politicians must generate the political will to cut programs[.]"[2]

With the second cost-cutting method, leaders may demand across-the-board cuts and nitpick each and every line item, somehow hoping the nickels and dimes saved will make a difference. Chances are, they'll also create more hoops that bureaucrats will need to jump through if they want to spend any money in their budget. For example, we recall being required to get ministerial approval to spend a thousand dollars, even though we surmised it cost half of that to process the paperwork. Consider this approach death by a thousand cuts, and it will likely never address the big-ticket items that should be slashed.

As Savoie states, an obvious way to reduce costs is to cut programs. During our years of service, there was the obligatory program review cycle wherein bureaucrats were asked to identify programs that could be cut. Bureaucrats worked hard to protect their programs and knew how to put forward items for possible cutting that would be distasteful for politicians, with the hope they wouldn't call out the bluff. We called these items "baby seals," as in we considered them too endearing to eliminate. More often than not, these "baby seals" were protected because they were politically unacceptable cuts.

Examples that were held up during our time included the NS schooner "Bluenose," before it became a boondoggle. Many will argue that should have made it to the cutting room floor long before its latest incarnation set sail. Local museums were a perennial favourite in NS; we assumed this was the case in other provinces as well. Most politicians wouldn't touch these institutions, even though there was evidence in some cases of only four visitors a week. Museums and other cultural institutions generally do not pay for themselves, and bureaucrats held these up because they knew politicians recognized their value to communities. This worked over the years; we can't recall a local museum ever being shut down as a means of cost control or reduction.

This leads us to an observation Hennebury shared with us:

While the practice of accounting between public and private sectors are quite similar, how we use and make decisions with it are quite different. I was listening one evening to a discussion on CBC radio about the use of science in public policy. I drew an analogy to accounting. The speaker made the point that politicians are elected to make decisions and while science should inform those decisions, science is not the decision. Accounting is similar. For example, accounting may tell us, from a pure numbers perspective, that we shouldn't operate museums. They don't (generally) operate in a balance let alone a surplus, so therefore we should close them. Can you imagine a Canada without museums (or monuments)? Public policy is informed by accounting in this case, but accounting does not make the decision, people do. That's one reason governing is so tough; not everyone will agree with that decision, but at least everyone can be informed by it and know what it costs.

Because all governments will always be looking for ways to reduce spending, bureaucrats are advised to make program review an ongoing part of managing finite resources, and to continue making the case to reduce or cut programs that are no longer working as intended. Financial services staff can help with this work, including costing out alternatives; identifying other streams of revenue; as well as sharing knowledge about possible restrictions or limitations on the funding available. However, it is critical to recognize that politicians ultimately make the decisions on what or whether to cut.

One area where politicians no longer hesitate to make cuts is civil service positions because they know there is not a lot of public support for the bureaucracy. The government of Alberta was the latest in a long line to issue letters to their unions in advance of bargaining for 2020 collective agreements outlining potential cuts that would impact 2,500 positions across several ministries. We shared more about this trend in

Chapter 2, with many seeing the civil service as a drain on the economy. Over the years, governments have also reduced some of the benefits that employees used to receive, which happened in the private sector long before hitting public sector employees. Some of those benefits included public service awards upon retirement for years of service; and extending the time needed to qualify for early retirement. There was citizen and private industry support alike for these actions, which we are sure gave the government of the day confidence to make these cuts.

Year-end spending

Another pattern, at least in NS, is the year-end spending bonanzas, which still existed during our time, despite efforts to curtail them. Managers who didn't spend all the money they were allocated in a given year feared losing it or being criticized for not forecasting accurately — now there's a contradiction! This resulted in little motivation to try to save for upcoming obligations in the following year. We knew many managers who tried to save money because they were aware their costs to provide the same level of service would go up the next year, but alas, it was taken from them, despite their foresight. Hennebury told us "the fear is often greater than the reality. But the fear makes people act. It's something that needs to be recognized by both spenders and guardians."

The unknown unknowns

We also want to flag the unknown unknowns. As everyone knows from managing a personal budget, both internal and external factors can have an impact on how well you are able to stick to it. Lawsuits, in particular, are on the rise, requiring governments to pay out because of poor decision making or outright negligence. In NS alone, the more prominent and egregious suits include institutional abuse at the Home for Colored Children, which was settled in 2014, and the Shelburne School for Boys in the early 1990s. There is also the wrongful murder conviction of Glen Assoun, whose lawyer said in 2019 they will seek a multi-million-dollar settlement. At the time of writing, provincial governments, including

NS and Ontario, are facing class-action lawsuits alleging negligence in addressing the spread of COVID-19 in long-term care facilities. Federally, there is the reconciliation process to address the harm and impact of residential schools on Indigenous peoples, as well as individual cases such as Omar Khadr, who sued government for infringing on his *Charter* rights, which was settled in 2017. These are just a few of the often-unexpected financial pressures governments face that impact the ability for all governments and bureaucrats to stay on track.

Another significant liability that continues to grow relates to mitigating the effects associated with climate change. We've all seen increases in the severity and frequency of natural disasters, including floods, drought, fires, hurricanes and winter storms. Pandemic-related interventions also used up significant resources from government coffers. Consider that the federal government alone approved the spending of $200 billion in federal aid in July 2020.

And of course, like clockwork, in our time, departments in the NS government were often called on, sometime after December, to contribute 5 per cent of their budget to cover overruns at the Department of Health.

Chasing the ace

Switching to patterns on the revenue side of the house, governments at different levels also go looking for money from one another. Municipalities look to provincial bodies, and provincial bodies most often knock on the door of their federal partners. These requests often result in cost-sharing endeavours. This practice is one way to leverage money needed to fund projects.

We called this the bureaucratic version of "chasing the ace." Bureaucrats with a program or idea that needed funding support tried to hook up with a federal-provincial-territorial (FPT) working group connected to their work. There are hundreds of groups on the go at any one time. Be warned, however; these groups work slowly, but if patience can be applied, the payoff can be well worth it. Departments across all jurisdictions have dozens and dozens of agreements that have arisen from these tables, including shared capital projects, shared funding for not-for-profit and corporate initiatives, as well as shared support to individuals in many areas of need. Most agreements come with expiration dates so there are ongoing efforts to renegotiate. The Canadian Intergovernmental Conference Secretariat tracks the broad scope of work that takes place at various FPT tables.[3] The agency provides administrative support and planning services for meetings of ministers and deputy ministers throughout Canada, as well as posts formal communiqués and documentation arising from the discussions.

Despite the painfully slow pace of these table discussions and negotiations, taking part in creating national programs is an important role for governments, bureaucrats and for the country as a whole. If provinces do not or cannot play because of fiscal constraints, they will lose out on possible funding. This can weaken the connections that form from working together, which helps unite the country as a whole. In other words, it is to the provinces' advantage to play nice with their federal counterparts.

We hope this account has given you a greater appreciation of the scope of government spending and the work that goes into managing it. As we noted in our introduction, money makes government work; there is a lot at stake. We know there are many bureaucrats working hard to manage this process for the benefit of citizens.

Case in Point

As we have already mentioned, one of the more dramatic cuts we were required to orchestrate — while still small in the grand scheme of things — involved a decision to close an "arm's length" arts council. It followed an across-the-board directive requiring all departments and agencies to cut 5 per cent from the budget. When the directive to cut was issued, the arts council launched a "Save our Arts Council" campaign, in effect biting the hand that fed it by suggesting the government was trying to dismantle the organization, which was not the government's intention. Media picked up the hype, reporting that the government was putting the arts in jeopardy. And while most commentary supported the council, some spoke out suggesting the council was a closed shop with awards and grants going to the same established artists and groups.

The campaign may have attracted public support, but it also had unintended consequences, including drawing scrutiny from within the bureaucracy. A review of spending revealed the council spent almost 30 per cent of the money it was supposed to be distributing to artists and arts organization on administration — a higher ratio than employees offering similar services within the department responsible for overseeing the agency. Government cited administrative costs as a factor in its decision to close the council.

This case raises a few points worthy of review. The first is that when governments issue directives associated with across-the-board cuts, current recipients would be well advised not to take it personally. The arts council's response drew attention to their operations and resulted in a closer look at how they were managing government money. This did not serve them well. Another point is that had government been paying attention all along and undertaking regular program reviews, the high administrative costs would have been caught long before.

TALKING POINTS
- Bureaucrats manage considerable wealth on the public's behalf.
- Both elected officials and bureaucrats are bound by legislation that dictates how money is managed and spent, and there are many checks and balances in place.
- Cost cutting is a continuous process in government. If you're lucky enough to control a budget, be ready to defend how you've spent every penny. And for those who may have to publicly account for spending, don your armour and be prepared to face criticism.
- Budgets can make or break governments. The exercise is taken very seriously and should be given all that is at stake.
- Financial services employees can be allies, so work on developing and maintaining positive relationships.

- While governments may not know the specifics, there will always be unknowns that will place pressure on government's ability to meet their financial goals.

Don't take our word for it

Savoie writes:

> From time to time, citizens will get a glimpse of waste in govern-
> ment when a financial audit reports that someone broke the rules
> or when the results of an access-to-information request uncovers
> financial or administrative abuses. It will be recalled, for example,
> that the auditor general revealed in 2001 that the federal govern-
> ment had sent home-heating cheques to 1,600 prison inmates
> and a year later declared that senior bureaucrats had broken 'just
> about every rule in the book' in mismanaging the Chrétien govern-
> ment's sponsorship program. Such incidents are widely reported
> in the media, and they give bureaucracy a bad name. But they are
> often isolated cases and represent a minuscule amount of the gov-
> ernment expenditure budget. In any event, they can never tell the
> whole story of how government decides and why. Often they speak
> to the problem, not to the cause."[4]

Chapter 8

WE'LL GET BACK TO YOU ON THAT

*"Open Government is like the live theatre: in order to have
something to show openly there must first be much hidden
activity. And all sorts of things have to be cut or altered in
rehearsals, and not shown to the public until you have got
them right."*

— Sir Humphrey Appleby, *Yes Minister*

IN THIS CHAPTER:
- The World of Government Research
- Collecting and Using Government Information
- Challenges Bureaucrats Face When Gathering or Using Research
- Research Outside of Government's Walls

We've titled this chapter in honour of a frequently used phrase in the
research world that is shared by bureaucrats. Questions we couldn't
answer came from leaders, stakeholders, media and citizens alike. While
there may be times when the response was used as a delay tactic, we've
been in many situations where the need for more research was legitimate.

We were never researchers in the strict sense of the term, but we were
required to pull together information or to oversee the research needed
to support decision making and respond to information requests from
a variety of sources. This included working with Statistics Canada
information to produce reports on the implications associated with
their studies for our jurisdiction. We also scoured through information

collected within our own and within other departments to respond to inquiries. In some cases, we issued requests for proposals for researchers to conduct studies on a department's behalf. Other times, we planned and compiled information from consultations or conducted jurisdictional reviews and case studies to shed light on a question or problem leaders were trying to solve.

We're dedicating a chapter to research because governments have invested heavily in building research capacity within the civil service. These investments include developing and maintaining thousands of information systems, hiring and training employees to gather, input and analyze data, as well as contracting with researchers, pollsters, academics and others to produce and support research.

In this chapter, we'll take a look at the world of government research, and we'll share insights on some of the methods bureaucrats use to gather information. We'll also share some challenges with traditional research methods, along with frustrations we faced when undertaking work in the research sphere.

The World of Government Research

We'll begin with the basics to make things clear. For the purposes of this chapter, research refers to efforts by bureaucrats to collect and study information to draw conclusions that can help support government action or respond to inquiries from the public in all its guises. The world of government research also includes efforts to encourage, influence and sponsor studies in the wider world, which we will address at the end of the chapter.

To put the importance of research in perspective, consider examples from our personal lives. It's safe to assume most of us conduct research on a regular basis. We look for evidence, obtained through research, to help us decide what type of car to buy, who we should insure it with, where the best place is to get maintenance done and, eventually, determine the best price for resale once we're finished with it. This is done over and over again for just about any major purchase, but also for many life decisions, such as what neighbourhood to live in and where we would like to go on vacation. The information we gather gives us comfort that we are making an informed decision.

We expect you can appreciate the value of research to inform your own decisions. Thankfully, this activity goes on in government workplaces, with many bureaucrats working to help make sense of questions or problems governments have to address. In most cases, research forms the basis for decisions regarding government policies, programs and services. Yes, it can be a long, drawn-out process, but the alternative of no research would be unthinkable. Imagine a world where politicians simply made decisions based on their instincts, likely political; using their education and experience, which is limited in some cases; or good judgement, but sadly, some have none.

Should you be wondering who actually conducts this research, it may surprise you to learn there are thousands of people doing this work every day in government departments across the country. It may also surprise you to read that these bureaucrats are engaging, interesting, creative and personable people. This description likely flies in the face of the stereotypical researcher that many imagine. You know ... the ones with glasses, faces buried in a book and spouting statistics as the eyes of those around them glaze over. It's also important to point out the work they do is most often interesting, informative and challenging.

Many of these people reside in departmental research and policy shops with system support from information technology staff. While the employees in these shops are experts in the field, civil servants throughout the system often play a key role in the research process. This includes providing data about their programs, generating information through literature and case file reviews or providing financial information. People who conduct research in government aren't always called "researchers"; they can be referred to as statisticians, mathematicians or analysts as well.

To add credibility to our suggestion that many of these people are not hiding away in some office alone and buried in paperwork, in almost every jurisdiction, there are policy tables, forums and committees — all searching for or reviewing evidence that will help governments make informed, and hopefully better, decisions.

A wealth of information assets

Because of the government research work undertaken, decision makers, stakeholders and citizens have access to a wealth of information assets. We expect most readers have heard of Statistics Canada. This national office undertakes research on all aspects of Canadian society, generating countless data sets and producing thousands of analytical reports. While Statistics Canada may be the mothership in the government's world of research, there are many more informative resources available within other federal agencies and at the provincial and municipal levels of government.

Some common government information sources include population statistics gathered through the census and employment rates gathered through labour market surveys. There is information on consumer spending and exports, as well as volunteer activities and recreational participation rates. Others include criminal justice indictors, wait times for health services, as well as motor vehicle accidents, births, deaths, police complaints and tourism visits, to name a few of the thousands of data sources held by government.

We would be hard-pressed to suggest that governments don't produce enough data. Consider the federal government's open data initiative alone, which boasts more than 80,000 information assets available.[1] Provincial governments also have their own assets, including NS.[2] The site lists 586 data sets covering social services, business and the economy, government administration, and nature and the environment. The most accessed records at the time we checked included crown land; municipal property tax rates; government pay scales; and crime statistics. Ontario also has an open data initiative with 2,700 data sets noted.[3]

The challenge for us — and anybody else accessing government information — was figuring out who had the information, mining through it and trying to make sense of it all. A lot of government data is focused on a narrow issue or slice of government business and is scattered throughout various federal and provincial departments and agencies.

Collecting and Using Government Information

To help navigate government data sources, it may help to know there are two types of research we dealt with on a regular basis. We will be limiting our comments to our experience as bureaucrats using government data, but we hope the insights we share will help anybody interested in this work.

The first type of data is qualitative, which is research conducted to obtain non-numerical information. Examples of work in this area could be conducting interviews to get a sense of people's feelings, ideas or experiences usually through broad and open-ended questions. It often includes human contact, offers a more holistic perspective and may involve groups. The second category is quantitative research, which is all about numbers that rely on somebody somewhere tracking incidences, quantities or rates. Closed-ended questionnaires can fall into this camp, because while people may be giving their opinion, it is based on a predetermined list of options, and their responses can be quantified with others.

To illustrate how we used both qualitative and quantitative data, we'll share an example involving a comprehensive analysis of youth crime in NS. The research report was submitted as part of a 2006 commission of inquiry into the youth criminal justice system. The commission examined the circumstances in which 52-year-old Theresa McEvoy was killed when her car was broadsided by a stolen vehicle driven by a serial young offender. The young offender had been released from jail, despite having dozens of outstanding criminal charges pending against him.

The research report included quantitative data and analysis, including a detailed statistical review of youth criminal activity, as well as a statistical review of how young offenders were being dealt with, including sentencing outcomes. On the qualitative side, the report included a summary of issues identified by provincial government officials and others providing youth services, which were obtained through interviews. Beyond those two types of data sources, the report was supplemented with additional research on risk and protective factors for youth crime; developmental theories of delinquent behaviour; and a jurisdictional review of successful intervention/prevention practices.

Another example where we used both quantitative and qualitative data to inform action involved work for a NS minister's task force on safer streets and communities. Quantitative data was used to set the context, including distributing geographically specific crime statistics to those participating in the consultation process. On the qualitative side, focus groups were held throughout the province with key experts, including educators, social workers, lawyers and police, followed by public town hall sessions in the evening. Policy analysts were on hand for the sessions to capture feedback for analytical purposes. Feedback was then analyzed, and a report produced to inform the efforts of the task force.

Lies, damn lies and statistics

In these situations, we were fortunate. There was a wealth of quantitative data available regarding the areas of study and a commitment from decision makers to invest resources into gathering the information needed to do a thorough analysis. But that is not always the case.

The fact is much of the data government departments produce is quantitative in nature. Aspects of issues are broken down into measurable bits, and then systems are set up to capture the data, which is then analyzed and summarized to inform discussion or a decision. The data produced is especially useful for identifying shifts and patterns in trends over time. However, such data and analysis will rarely point the way towards specific actions governments can take to change course or address an entrenched issue, which is why more robust research is often needed.

The focus on quantitative data is understandable. Many find comfort in the certainty of numbers. But data is prone to imperfection. Numbers are easily misinterpreted or misused, hence the popular statement: "There are three kinds of lies: lies, damned lies and statistics."

On the survey side of things, it's been our experience that many in government use simplistic approaches that include scales or a series of multiple-choice questions. In these surveys, the "right" answer — namely, the one the sponsor is hoping for — is often apparent and the questions are presented without context. Quite often the most appropriate answer is likely "it depends," but that is not often given as a choice.

Most employee surveys we participated in fell into this trap. We expect it's the same in other organizations. The surveys were a snapshot in time, and we knew responses could be heavily influenced by anything that happened prior to filling it out. For example, if our boss just placed a pile of work on our plate, chances are we were in a bad mood, and our responses to work questions reflected these feelings.

You may be thinking, so what? It would be one thing if the results were simply shared for all to take or leave. But unfortunately, the data collected and analyzed from these simplistic tools are used to shape policy and action. In the case of employee surveys, which are undertaken by governments throughout the country, senior leaders were required to act on issues of concern identified in the surveys. Some of the issues may have stemmed from many people having a bad day before filling out the survey. As an example, engagement became a huge focus of senior management energy after dismal results from the employee surveys undertaken in NS. Departments struck employee-management committees who met regularly to explore ways to engage. Our inboxes filled with messages from leaders; websites were set up; and regular employee meetings were scheduled to share information. Engagement suggests a two-way street, but the initiatives were usually one-way communication masked as engagement. The efforts appeared disingenuous to us. We found ourselves mentally checking out, which is the exact opposite of what leaders were hoping we would do.

Polling is another simplistic approach overly used in government research efforts, which most often consists of closed-ended questions designed to capture respondents' opinion. We conceived of an interesting research project: gather all the questions government departments pose annually in these surveys, analyze them and examine the data, which would ultimately point to what opinions governments are most concerned with in any given year. Low and behold, we discovered the federal government produces an annual report of its public opinion research activities. For the fiscal year 2018–19, the federal government conducted 147 public opinion activities at a cost of $15.3 million and involved 35 departments. Most of these studies involved quantitative research (52 per cent), followed by qualitative research (26 per cent) with the remaining being a combination of both (22 per cent).[4]

We were involved in crafting many questions for the omnipresent "Omnibus Survey" courtesy of Corporate Research Associates here in NS. The company has since changed its name to Narrative Research. We expect there are similar favourite pollsters in all provinces. For example, Alberta has a public opinion research policy and maintains a list of pre-qualified public opinion research vendors. We found studies from Harris/Decima and Environics Research Group, to name two. Most recently, the Ontario Public Service Employees Union retained Nanos to undertake polling among Ontarians on the priorities for the provincial government after COVID-19.

Many bureaucrats throughout the land likely spend countless hours quantifying results from various polls year after year. In one case, we tried to convince decision makers that asking a particular series of questions annually wasn't necessary, especially because Statistics Canada produced similar metrics — mind you, they only asked them every four years. The department in question had been paying thousands of dollars annually to ask these questions, and employees spent hours and hours poring over the results to share with decision makers. The results rarely changed from year to year, which was not that surprising, since opinions rooted in values about social issues tend to remain fairly consistent for most people. Some might say that amounted to a significant waste of time and money.

As an aside, while working for government, we were not able to participate in the polls when we got the calls at home because pollsters usually asked if we worked for government. Now that we've retired, we've had a chance to respond to a few such polls and took some joy pointing out flaws in the questions being asked, which didn't amuse the questioner.

One last point on polling. You'll often hear a passing reference to "margin of error." The larger the margin of error, the less confidence one should have that the poll results are a "true" representation of the opinion of the population. We recommend paying attention to the margin of error, especially if you're going to use the results for decision-making purposes.

Quality over quantity

On the qualitative side of the research house, efforts to gather information from people can be more expensive. It also requires reaching out to others with knowledge about the problem or issue. As noted, governments occasionally don't wish to draw attention to issues they are grappling with.

Opposition parties are the first to demand ministers undertake consultation, which is a form of qualitative research. They often take great pleasure in cherry-picking public feedback that supports their particular stand on an issue. However, we did notice that once these same opposition parties attained power, they quickly retreated from their desire for more engagement. There's a good reason for their aversion; such efforts can make governing parties uncomfortable when the feedback is not aligned with what they had hoped.

Consider an example where a new party upon coming to power in NS shut down a veritable institution that engaged citizens on a wide range of issues for decades and produced recommendations for government's consideration. While in opposition, that same party extolled the virtues of this unique entity, Voluntary Planning. Operating independently from government with a volunteer board of directors and a few paid employees, it provided a forum to explore policy issues without the direct influence of political or partisan considerations. It also built credibility and trust with numerous organizations and individuals over the years.

In an op-ed piece that appeared in *The Chronicle Herald*, the then-deputy premier said: "by moving Voluntary Planning resources into a central agency, we are building new capacity to strengthen consultation practices[.]"[5] One of us worked in government during this time, and all government bureaucrats got out of the shutdown effort was a template. In its own editorial response titled "So much for openness," the newspaper slammed the decision: "... To its shame, the Dexter government is the first one in the board's half century of distinguished service to fire the messenger for not being 'in line with government thinking' ... What a slap in the face to public engagement and to all the good citizens who have put in unpaid service on Voluntary Planning committees and task forces over decades."[6] We couldn't have said it better ourselves.

This brings us to the reality that some governments are open to consultation and others are not. Our experience suggests most go from one extreme to the other. Somewhere in between would be ideal. That's because we recognize that while governments should want broad public involvement on some aspects of policy, they were elected to make decisions and can be held to account for those decisions.

Common approaches used to gather qualitative information from people include inviting expert opinions, hosting focus groups or public forums and conducting one-on-one interviews. We dealt with a few frustrations on the qualitative data front and highlight them here.

The cult of the expert

Sometimes senior leaders hand-picked a few experts to offer an opinion on a complex course of action, leaving people with direct experience out of the knowledge-gathering discussions. This often led to disappointment from those who wanted to participate in the process. We're not saying expert opinion isn't valuable, but it, too, has limits. We recall a few cases where expert opinion failed to take into account operational realities, and the recommended course of action was completely unrealistic. Had those with hands-on experience been asked to participate during the research stage, the implementation issues would have been caught early on.

Capture by special interest groups

Closely linked to the above was not reaching out wide enough or allowing an appropriate amount of time for people to participate in research efforts. Complacency and alienation can impact participation by those who don't have a vested stake or personal interest in the outcome. Few people took part in consultations out of purely altruistic concern for others.

It was therefore critical to cast the net wide, otherwise results could be easily swayed by those who have a vested interest in the issue. This can result in decisions favouring the few and not the many.

Think-tanks
Another area of frustration for us was the credence given to some think-tanks over others, depending on the ideological bent of whatever party was in power. For those unaware, think-tanks are organized groups of so-called experts who produce research and market their advice and ideas on specific political, economic or social problems.

As bureaucrats, we quickly learned governments tend to favour research from outsiders, especially think-tanks. The public and media seem to soak it up as well. Sure, think-tanks have their place, but many people may not consider that such groups work for a special interest and not necessarily the public interest. Here's our handy reference of distinction regarding major ones:

- For the "market is good" and "government is bad" choir, we were familiar with the Fraser Institute and AIMS (they merged in 2019), the Business Council on National Issues, the CD Howe Institute and the Canadian Taxpayers Federation. The latter bureaucracy-basher often "scolds government for dubious spending, but keeps its own books tightly shut."[7]
- We found left-wing leanings at the Centre for Policy Alternatives, the Caledon Institute and the Canadian Labour Congress.
- Somewhere in the middle there is the Conference Board of Canada, the Canadian Centre for Management Development and the Canadian Policy Research Network.
- From legal experts and human rights advocates, we were aware of the Law Commission of Canada, as well as various provincial law commissions, and the Canadian Centre for Law and Democracy.
- And, of course, there are numerous academic bodies and professors offering up their research.

There are many more, so we always did a bit of research on whatever think-tank study we came across to place *their* research in context. This ensured we were aware of the inherent biases they may have had.

Challenges Bureaucrats Face When Gathering or Using Research

We hope you have a better sense of the types of data governments collect and use to inform action. We now address some challenges we faced when trying to use the results of the research gathered.

Limited capacity to consume research

Even when governments and bureaucrats have the relevant quantitative and qualitative data needed to more fully understand an issue, some leaders and decision makers are simply not well prepared to consume such research. They may lack the ability to process information that conflicts with their preconceived notions, or there simply is not enough time to fully comprehend the results of the research. In those cases, bureaucrats are blamed unnecessarily. Sadly, we both witnessed some cases where politicians blamed others to avoid the embarrassment of admitting they didn't understand the evidence.

Ray MacNeil, a 26-year veteran of NS public service who spent many years exploring advances in the complexity sciences and their application to improved public services, shared the following with us: "Contrary to popular belief, access to data and capability to create analytic products is not always the problem for governments ... it's also the inability of decision makers to consume the analysis created for them and to synthesize it with other knowledge, experience and perspectives. This is a skillset unto itself that is not always recognized as such."

Disregarding evidence that doesn't align with ideology

Thankfully, we didn't face the following challenge often, but there were cases where those in power disregarded knowledge gained through study that didn't support their ideological positions. Some take it to a new level of low. We would place all political climate change deniers in this camp. Shari Graydon, writing for the *Globe and Mail*, admonished this practice; and while the article is dated to 2010, her points are worth repeating. She writes:

> Is it too much to expect my governments — supported by one of the best-educated and most-respected civil services in the world (not to mention my tax dollars) — to rely on reputable research when making major spending and policy decisions on my behalf? I don't think so. I understand that studies are sometimes contradictory, that methodology must be rigorous, that statistics can lie. But I also understand the value of disinterested investigation, the power of aggregated research, and the benefits of multi-disciplinary approaches to assessing problems ...
> Take the get-tough-on-crime legislation — please. A doubling of expenditures on prisons — almost \$2-billion over five years — to incarcerate more people at a time when crime rates are falling and the U.S. experiment reveals the practice to be demonstrably ineffective. Follow that with the unwillingness to recognize, let alone attempt to address, the undeniable and potentially significant impacts of climate change (regardless of what's causing them).[8]

When we found ourselves in situations where evidence was being ignored, we still tried to get decision makers to take a second look. But at the end of the day, we knew the decisions were not ours to make.

Confirmation bias

Closely related to the above is confirmation bias, which refers to the tendency to selectively search for and favour information that confirms one's beliefs. It has significant ramifications for public policy research. It tends to flourish when everybody around thinks alike. As lawyer Twila Reid notes for *Canadian Lawyer*, "confirmation bias is a serious problem that has been linked to climate change denial, anti-vaccine beliefs, flawed police investigations and wrongful convictions. Its reach travels further than the moon and even invades politics and law firms. Confirmation bias flourishes when decision-makers are all like-minded people coming from like-minded backgrounds with like-minded experiences (as they are likely to have the same pre-existing beliefs)."[9] When we engaged in research, we tried to keep our own biases in check and continually challenged our assumptions, and we encouraged others to do the same. We also worked hard to ensure those with diverse education, skills and experiences were engaged in our projects.

State secrets

Another issue worthy of mention within the bureaucracy itself is the potential to spin research study results or to not release them at all. Consider this NS example, which has an important lesson. Toby Mendel, with The Centre for Law and Democracy, wrote about a NS civil servant justifying the decision to withhold release of a $140,000 taxpayer-funded study on gambling, claiming the report wouldn't be helpful to make informed decisions.[10]

The minister at the time also claimed there was nothing to release because the report was "a failed work in progress." Mendel noted that "these claims miss the point. The public's right to access information should not depend on a paternalistic assessment by government officials of how useful the information might or might not be."

A related issue concerns the barriers to obtaining government information. For the most part, governments pick and choose what they want to release. If people want access to information that governments don't want them to have, they may well have to apply for it through freedom of information laws.

These laws allow anyone to request records owned by a government or a public institution. Those who are persistent and have deep pockets can likely get access to the information they seek, unless the information falls into certain categories that are exempt. These categories include information that would constitute advice to elected officials; fall under solicitor-client privilege; jeopardize safety; breach a third-party's privacy rights; or, in the case of business, jeopardize their competitive advantage.

Navigating freedom of information laws can be frustrating for those seeking the information and time consuming and intimidating for bureaucrats when they are requested to turn over files relating to a particular application. These requests are usually submitted by the opposition or the press, both of whom know how and where to dig for information.

It can also be embarrassing if it involves turning over something a bureaucrat wishes they never wrote. However, if a bureaucrat has gone through the exercise once, they will likely forever use that as a filter when crafting correspondence and advice.

Research Outside of Government's Walls

We mentioned in the introduction that governments also encourage, influence and fund research studies. That includes funding studies through expressions of interest or providing funding to research institutes and organizations. Our experience in this area is limited, but we want to acknowledge it because we're thankful investments are being made to expand knowledge and understanding. In that regard, more is better.

One of us had a positive experience wherein the government partnered with academic and private industry partners on a four-year research project. We mentioned this project in Chapter 4 when discussing challenges associated with being the first jurisdiction to take action on an issue. It was the largest study of its kind in Canada. The project's objective was to determine the economic impact of developing and implementing a healthy workplace program and involved hundreds of public servants. Results demonstrated that employees working in a healthy culture had a positive impact on the organization's bottom line. The study provided evidence to support investments in employees' health, and the findings could be applied to any workplace, whether public, private or not-for-profit.

We were also involved in government efforts to fund research to improve the operations of various not-for-profit organizations that make valuable contributions within communities. Because they operate on tight budgets, most not-for-profits would be hard-pressed to fund such research. As an example, NS contracted researchers to assess whether a theatre group had appropriate systems, policies and programs in place to carry out their mandate, which included providing a platform for culturally diverse talents. The study helped the organization improve its governance and management, thereby benefiting the cultural sector as a whole.

In another case, Nova Scotia's Department of Justice contracted an external research firm to assess the effectiveness of the province's *Domestic Violence Intervention Act*. The act allows a victim of domestic violence to apply for an emergency protection order in cases where they cannot wait to obtain an appropriate remedy from the courts. If granted, the victim can secure a number of conditions, such as temporary possession of a home or a requirement that the person accused of domestic violence stay away from the victim or home. In that case, we had lots of statistical data available, including the number of requests received; the number of orders granted; the numbers revoked; the number of requests varied and so forth. However, we didn't have the qualitative data needed to assess whether the tool was working as intended and being used appropriately, which required reaching out to those using it, as well as those responsible for overseeing the legislation. The completed research study was used to inform policy and programming changes.

We'll close this chapter with a shout-out to all the researchers in government offices throughout the country. Without their work, the evidence needed to support decision making wouldn't exist. And despite the stereotypes, we will restate this work is often interesting, exciting, creative, challenging and necessary.

Case in Point

Because research can be a heavy topic, this case in point falls on the lighter side of things. Consider a farcical example of how drawing on numbers for policy decisions can go sideways. In essence, referendums are a form of quantitative research. You ask a question and count the results. The case we're talking about involves a rant by Rick Mercer on *This Hour Has 22 Minutes* during the 2000 federal election campaign. Former Canadian Alliance leader Stockwell Day had proposed referendums could be triggered on any subject if a petition was able to collect 350,000 signatures of voting age citizens. In response, Mercer asked viewers to sign a petition on the show's website that asked Day to change his name to Doris Day, after the American actor and singer. The petition purportedly garnered over 1,200,000 online votes, and the stunt generated a great deal of publicity. In response to the show segment, Day responded with "… Que será, será."[11]

Halifax-based Geoff D'Eon, an award-winning television producer, helped to produce this segment for *This Hour Has 22 Minutes*. We asked him what he learned from it and if he had any advice for people who might want to rely on such numbers for major policy decisions in the future. He said: "This was an early example of people-power harnessed via the internet. To the casual observer, Day's referendum policy might have looked like democracy in action. But clearly, it was poorly thought out. The triggering threshold was way too low. Referenda are expensive! Beware the politician or bureaucrat who serves up half-baked ideas, especially when there are satirists about. What Rick did was recognize the pomposity and ridiculousness of this political trial balloon, and so he put a pin in it. The resulting bang was hilarious. Everybody laughed. The policy was dead on arrival, and everybody moved on."

TALKING POINTS

As in previous chapters, repeat after us:

- Governments invest heavily in research, with thousands of bureaucrats throughout the country involved in producing evidence to inform decision making.
- There is a massive amount of federal, provincial and municipal government data available, but figuring out how to mine and make sense of it can be challenging.

- To get the best results from research, a mix of quantitative and qualitative data is needed.
- Polls and simplistic surveys are snapshots in time and context specific, and therefore have limited use.
- When engaging with others to gather information, it is critical to be aware of biases and seek out a variety of sources.
- There are limits to how bureaucrats can make best use of the research they've gathered. They are not the owners of the research produced, nor the ones deciding if they'll act on the research results.
- Take heed from this quote by Dr. Martin Luther King, Jr. who said: "Knowledge is a process of piling up facts. Wisdom lies in their simplification."[12]

Don't take our word for it

We appreciate — and hope you will, too — the following observations made by Andrea Jones-Rooy: "Data is an imperfect approximation of some aspect of the world at a certain time and place. It's what results when humans want to know something about something, try to measure it, and then combine those measurements in particular ways." She identifies four ways that we can introduce imperfections into data, including: random errors; systematic errors; errors of choosing what to measure; and errors of exclusion. "These errors don't mean that we should throw out all data ever and nothing is knowable, however. It means approaching data collection with thoughtfulness, asking ourselves what we might be missing, and welcoming the collection of further data."[13]

Chapter 9
SPINNING A YARN

*"The purpose of minutes is not to record events, it is to protect
people. Minutes are there to reflect what people thought they
should have said, with the benefit of hindsight."*

— Sir Humphrey Appleby, *Yes Minister*

IN THIS CHAPTER:
- Everyone Is In on the Game
- Centrally Speaking
- Fallouts from Central Control over Government Communications
- Stumbling Blocks to Getting the Message Out

We couldn't resist the temptation to title this last chapter after a
common perception that government communications are all about
spinning the truth. Yes, we know; governments can tell half-truths,
and when they do, it's likely because they want to convince citizens of
one thing or to avoid the consequences of something else.

However, that shouldn't take away from the fact that government
communications are a critical function. It is how citizens learn about
programs and services that will benefit them; how laws might affect them;
and what their elected officials are doing for them. Closely related to
communications are the social marketing efforts governments undertake
to tackle problems and influence behaviour in public policy areas such
as health, public safety and environmental protection. Examples include
campaigns to tackle smoking, prevent problem gambling, stop impaired
driving and encourage waste reduction, to name a few.

When you get right down to it, communications are a fundamental aspect of every activity we covered in this book. Communication efforts influence the culture of government organizations; are at the heart of relationship building; play a leading role in planning and policy development; and are an essential element in programming, budgeting and research. In this chapter, we'll be homing in on the function of communications, as well as specific activities undertaken and why government communications is fraught with difficulties. We'll also share some observations about issues that affected our efforts to communicate.

Everyone Is In on the Game

Almost every bureaucrat plays a role in government communications whether they realize it or not. Their approach and attitude can influence the perceptions people have about government programs and services. One of the more common complaints is that communications from governments are usually a long time coming. This is one area where bureaucrats and the public can agree. During our tenure, we, too, were recipients of government communications that were too little, too late.

In spite of such delays, we want to recognize the many valiant efforts bureaucrats throughout all levels of government make to communicate with citizens day in and day out. There are thousands and thousands of bureaucrats interacting one-on-one with a myriad of clients and stakeholders on any given day. Many of those communications have a direct and positive impact on the health and well-being of public service recipients.

For the most part, we believe bureaucrats are helpful and approach their job with professionalism, positivity and integrity. But we also understand that if bureaucrats are grumpy or lack knowledge about a particular policy or program, it will reflect negatively on a government as a whole. Unfortunately, we knew many people who formed a negative impression after just one bad experience, despite countless positive interactions with bureaucrats beforehand.

In addition to the daily interactions bureaucrats have with recipients of government services, there are many other bureaucrats working behind the scenes, crafting correspondence to individual citizens and processing information or service requests where attention to detail is critical and sloppy efforts don't cut it. Citizens and stakeholders write to politicians for a multitude of reasons, and they expect a response. Elected officials know if they don't respond, it could impact their re-election chances. Of course, they don't actually write the responses. That task is left to bureaucrats, who draft responses for officials to sign.

Writing responses to ministerial correspondence is not always an easy task. Many times, the issues are complex and have no clear answers. To complicate matters, the responses citizens receive are often not what they want to hear, which requires an additional layer of tact and diplomacy. Getting information needed to respond to concerns can also take time, but the people waiting for a response want it quickly. There are also layers of approval with everyone taking a shot at the content, which lengthens the time citizens have to wait to hear back from ministers.

For those reasons alone, many bureaucrats we knew dreaded having to deal with ministerial correspondence. In our time, bright yellow sheets or blue folders landing on our desk signalled a piece of correspondence needing attention, and they were to be made an immediate priority. It didn't matter if we had other deadlines, projects or meetings to attend; responses took precedence and could eat up a fair piece of a workday if the issue was complicated. Even though this happened quite frequently, drafting ministerial responses was never listed in our annual or monthly work plans, which flies in the face of setting realistic work goals. While this example is from NS, most jurisdictions likely have similar processes and challenges associated with ministerial correspondence.

The everyday interactions and transactions between citizens and bureaucrats we described represent the bulk of government communications efforts. However, the communications activities that garner the most public attention are orchestrated by staff hired specifically to communicate on governments' behalf. Among other activities, these are the employees who issue news releases, manage social media activity, plan public events and craft speeches for senior management and elected officials to deliver to stakeholder groups.

Centrally Speaking

There are hundreds of these professional communicators within government bureaucracies, who sport titles such as officers, advisors, coordinators, specialists, managers and directors. They are responsible for drafting and approving external departmental communications plans. Therefore, they directly influence the timing and ways that policies, laws and decisions regarding programs and services are communicated, including the very words that come out of elected officials' mouths.

For the most part, we found that communicators primarily focused their efforts on media relations — be that traditional or social. They also planned events, as well as coordinated social marketing and advertising. Further, they offered expertise in the areas of writing, editing, graphic design, photography, printing and branding.

When we first joined the NS government, official communications functions also included services such as libraries and a bookstore, as well as public inquiry phone lines within departments, but over the years, many were quietly phased out.

Back then, departments hired their own communications employees. They were scattered throughout the system and had a direct reporting relationship with the deputy ministers of various departments. By the late 1990s and early 2000s, the centralization trend spread to this professional service as it did to human resources, finance and information technology. Functional service units were formed, and all communications employees were brought under one roof. They then reported directly through a central agency management structure that retained power and control over government-wide communications efforts.

We recall Alberta was one of the first provinces to go down the centralization route; the function was placed under the premier's office in the early 1990s. Critics argued it adopted a more political tone and became the propaganda arm of the premier's office. Ontario has a central "Cabinet Office Communications" function headed by a deputy minister with responsibility for overall government communications and setting policies and standards governing ministry communications branches.

Alex Marland, a professor with the Department of Political Science at Memorial University in Newfoundland, noted in 2016 that federally "… the public sector has for some time gravitated toward coordinated and centralized messaging. Top-down marketing coordination within government dates to 1960s' efforts to unify all points of contact.[1] Further, he wrote, "The role of central planning in government communications and the politicization of the public service increased during Stephen Harper's truncated decade in power[.]"[2] He also noted, "For reasons that are not clear, the concept of spin was not a focus of academic interest, and it remains understudied in Canada."[3]

In NS, the service unit was called Communications Nova Scotia. Individual employees were assigned to specific departments, where staff had reporting relationships with both the central agency brass and departmental officials. This created two direct lines of reporting. Such shared reporting relationships can get awkward if there are disagreements between those giving the marching orders, considering communications staff are stuck in the middle.

One of us worked in communications at the time. The switch to centralization had both pros and cons. On the positive side, centralization meant staff could move throughout the system more easily and they benefited from shared training and development opportunities, as well as consistent practices and processes regarding position titles and pay scales.

Centralization also made it easier for government to align communications activities with the priorities of elected officials. Some saw this as a good thing because it enabled governments to communicate with "one voice," ensuring consistency in messaging across the organization.

Of course, there was a downside; individual departments lost autonomy over their communications efforts. In effect, the central agency called almost all the shots. Within departments, we experienced many more back-and-forth situations with central communications staff and political masters. We found ourselves fighting for permission to share information, or enduring public criticism for not communicating enough. This was exhausting, frustrating and did nothing to help departmental relationships with stakeholders.

Even sharing facts became difficult. For example, if a bureaucrat got a fact-based question from the media or the opposition, they needed to get permission from central communications staff to share those facts.

Communicators were also moved around quite regularly, and that created extra work for departments. Many other staff had to repeatedly bring new employees responsible for communicating up to speed on departmental issues, programs and services, so they could carry out their work.

Power in the hands of a few

We noted earlier that government communications staff are responsible for planning and directing external communications. The nature of their position requires them to work closely with ministers and political staff, and this access gives them a lot of power to influence how issues are perceived and decisions communicated. Many have been accused of manipulating information to portray government in the best light possible, earning them the label of "spin doctors." The reality is, political considerations can and will influence how information is shaped and delivered.

While serving in a communications role, one of us recalls putting a halt to the release of a strategic plan for NS museums that had been months in the making and developed by both bureaucrats and key stakeholders within communities. Staff had intended to share the plan widely and forwarded a heads-up in order to ensure the minister would be prepared to address any questions. The plan was lofty, requiring significant injections of new funds in an era of cutbacks and with a wide range of implications for local museum sites, which were near and dear to many elected officials. Because none of the elected leaders had been briefed, nor was the department in a position to act on many of the recommendations due to financial constraints, we suggested the department put the plan on hold and postpone any communications regarding the initiative. The minister agreed, to the dismay of all who worked so hard to articulate a vision for the sector. In that case, the decision to halt communications had little to do with partisan interests and more to do with government's inability to deliver on the proposed plan.

Communications staff have also been labelled as gatekeepers because they manage the relationship between media and departments. They are responsible for processing media requests and they often act as spokespeople delivering official statements, which are carefully scripted.

One of us served as a spokesperson during our career. An especially difficult exchange concerning a hazardous waste site known as the Sydney Tar Ponds occurred during that time. The site on Cape Breton Island contained runoff from a decommissioned steel plant. Media outlets were all over the story and for good reason, considering this began after repeated failures by government to address the waste; vocal opposition to various clean up options; and ball tossing between levels of government on who would pick up the tab. This was on top of demands by residents to be relocated. It was a tough role to fill, as every message delivered was met with criticism and cynicism. We were accused of covering up government incompetence or hiding the real agenda. This was a relatively common reception most spokespeople received when making statements on difficult public issues, even though, in this case, we were trying to impartially share information about what was happening. "Don't shoot the messenger" was something we wanted the public to understand and respect.

For those who find themselves in this position, it's worth heeding more words by Aucoin: "It is one thing to impartially outline and explain a government's policy. It is quite another to function as a government's agent promoting its agenda."[4]

We were not aware of any formal rules clearly delineating where to draw those lines — which would likely be an impossible task — but we recall some heuristics, such as:

- Avoid sharing personal opinions regarding government decisions or defending them;
- Never attack the opposition;

- Refrain from the use of partisan statements, including referencing government by their party label;
- Restrict quotes by backbenchers in official news releases; and
- Avoid overt promotion of government accomplishments, especially during election campaigns.

Of course, leading up to a call for an election is a different matter, when one can expect a flurry of news releases extolling the virtues of government's actions and investments. We recall departments often being asked for lists of "good things going on" that would then become part of a communication plan for the week. Again, this describes the situation in NS, but such practices play out in jurisdictions across the country.

Fallouts from Central Control over Government Communications

Now that we've made you aware of central communications control, we will share a few fallouts from the tight grip that governments have developed and maintained over communications efforts.

Trust issues

The first is the slow and steady erosion of permission for bureaucrats — other than official spokespeople — to speak directly to media or in most public forums. This erosion of permission persisted during our years of service, no matter the political stripe.

As we've noted, all media inquiries were routed through communications staff, who decided how to respond in consultation with elected officials. Federally, restrictions regarding media interaction were especially apparent during the Harper years. Some bureaucrats described directives that limited permission to speak publicly, along with difficult approval procedures. This changed somewhat with the Trudeau government reaffirming the rights of some bureaucrats — namely Canada's scientists — to speak to the media about their research.

The practices of media gatekeeping and bureaucratic muzzling have undoubtedly contributed to the distrust people have for governments, which can make communications suspect and thus ineffective. Research consistently reported that many citizens distrust their civic institutions, including official spokespeople. We are aware people distrust governments for a lot of reasons, including a lack of belief in what government is telling them. Sadly, there is a basis for that. There are many controversies wherein the government involved did not act in the public interest, as well as examples where governments contradict themselves. For example, how many times have you heard governments say there isn't money available, only to discover millions of dollars invested in a politically popular project?

Keep it simple, stupid

Another influence from central communications was a fixation with key messages to feed the mass media machine. We were often asked to develop key messages associated with something we were working on, especially if the work was controversial and likely to garner media attention. Complex problems were whittled down into three short and preferably snappy lines that officials could deliver to the media with the hope of shaping public opinion. When the house was sitting, we were required to whip those lines out on a daily basis to cover a wide range of issues on the off chance the minister or premier would be questioned in the house or scrummed by the media afterwards. This was often an exercise in wordsmithing and could be frustrating because it was, and is, difficult to explain a complex issue with a sound bite. Many bureaucrats we knew found this work difficult; as a result, whittling down words usually fell to communications people. This, too, came with risks, as subtleties could easily be missed, resulting in a misrepresentation of an issue or opportunity, and thus detracting from what government was trying to do. The aim was, as always, to keep things simple.

A closely related issue is the desire by some politicians, and at times, senior leaders, to dumb things down. When framing issues or challenges, great effort was put into eliminating ambiguity and trying to make things as simple as possible. In some cases, those efforts were warranted if the intention was to help people understand. But some issues are complex and need to be recognized and treated as such. For such issues, people must appreciate that there is no quick fix and recognize everyone has a role to play in addressing them. In one instance, a deputy minister insisted we stop using the word "complex" when describing an issue. She saw everything in black and white, and expected us to come up with a simple solution. However, we stressed that because the issue was complex, we needed to engage many others. In the end, we won the battle; we did get to reach out to others to help address the issue.

We believe governments should have more faith in people in regards to handling complex discussions. Some leaders don't seem to recognize the general public is more informed, and in some cases, better educated, than at any other point in time. Because of this blind spot, many officials continue to talk down to people. This practice can backfire; if people are insulted, they may simply stop listening. Ultimately, this can impact citizen participation in democratic processes, including elections, which is an undesired outcome.

On the flip side, we have had to write materials in a manner that was more geared to a seventh-grader than an elected official. We mean no disrespect here, but in one situation, it was difficult to prepare speeches, briefing notes and other important and often complex materials using language that a minister could understand, read and pronounce. Thankfully, it didn't happen often. We and others in similar situations always tried to do it in a manner that didn't bring attention to the challenges ministers had in respect to comprehension and oral communication.

Less is not more

On the internal side of the house, communications within the NS bureaucracy also took a hit after centralization. Once upon a time, communications staff developed materials promoting the work of bureaucrats and led team-building exercises to encourage camaraderie and information-sharing. This was done to improve the work environment with the belief that engaged employees would deliver better public services. After centralization, responsibility for those activities fell to deputies and managers. Unfortunately, we knew some senior leaders who did not make it a priority, and there were others who did not have the necessary skills or time to be effective internal communicators. As a result, employee engagement took a back seat. Less information was shared about what colleagues were doing, and what departments were doing, for that matter. In extreme cases, employees read about a major initiative that would affect their work on behalf of citizens in the news or through their union, rather than through formal internal communications channels.

Bureaucrats in regional offices likely felt the impact the most. We were both aware of many instances when news about what was happening in departments never went beyond the walls of the head office. Understandably, some bureaucrats in regional offices felt left out, uninformed and often resentful. And it was especially disconcerting when they would hear about issues from a member of the public. This left them feeling embarrassed by their lack of information on a recent issue. These days, we like to think technology and a better understanding of the importance of internal communications have reduced such gaps in information-sharing.

Stumbling Blocks to Getting the Message Out

This brings us to stumbling blocks that can get in the way of governments' efforts to communicate. We addressed many throughout this book, but want to highlight a few others.

In the situation we described about internal communication, we think technology is helping staff receive timely access to information. The same can be said for citizens, who can easily obtain government information online, including getting the necessary paperwork they may need to apply for government programs and services. But technology has also had some negative impacts.

Technology shield

We witnessed a significant drop in face-to-face interactions with the public over the years and with our colleagues in the office next door. Even phone calls lessened as people turned to email, both of which eliminated the opportunity to develop personal relationships with clients and colleagues. Of course, one can easily argue technology has been a saving grace during the COVID-19 crisis. Government offices were shut down; the only interactions took place through the use of technology.

Like other organizations, efforts to streamline incoming calls from the public has also fallen prey to automated systems that offer a laundry list of menu options. We recall one case where callers had to wade through a menu of ten items when a new department implemented the system. When the announcement was made, the department rationalized it, stating they were doing what other government departments had done and claiming it would enable them to "focus our resources on our core business." We chuckled about that because the statement could be interpreted to mean talking to citizens was not part of the department's core business.

Not that long ago, people could walk into any NS government department, be greeted by a receptionist and receive information or be directed to other bureaucrats who could help them. Departments once published directories with the names, titles and phone numbers of people responsible for programs and services, making it fairly easy to find and reach individuals who could help with an issue. This is no longer the case. It can be argued there is no easy access to public servants in many jurisdictions. One difference we experienced in NS was at the municipal level of government, where access to public servants still exists with relative ease.

Departments also slowly replaced public greeting areas with automated security entrances and signs on the door with a list of people and phone numbers to call to gain admittance. Citizens lost access. Internally, many bureaucrats were impacted as well. This was due to how they often had to go to various departments for meetings. Upon arrival, they would scan the list of names and play a guessing game of who they needed to call to gain entry. In some cases, the person they were trying to call was waiting for them in a boardroom; as a result, they'd stand outside waiting for someone to come out and let them in.

We admit it sounds trivial, but there were a lot of meetings; if we added up all the minutes bureaucrats spent twiddling their thumbs waiting for entry, you might understand the frustration this caused.

The vast majority of the bureaucracy is behind a wall and shielded from the public. We received many calls from people who were angry and frustrated when they finally got through to us because they felt like they had been given the runaround. This made communication difficult, to say the least. This shielding trend was referenced in the *Financial Post*, with author Philip Cross pointing out that "Canada's civil service is increasingly isolated physically from the public it nominally serves. More and more, the civil service treats the public at best as an inconvenience and at worst a security threat. As the public's presence and voice fades from the bureaucrat's view, the isolation encourages the civil service to be captured by special interest groups or pursue its own interests."[5] We don't necessarily agree with his conclusion, but the potential is there.

Keeping things under wraps

In addition to building a wall, we've also noticed an increase in what some could label government secrecy. We talked about confidentiality requirements in an earlier chapter; however, for this discussion on communication, there is the added issue of solicitor-client privilege, which can be a cover for many a sin. Bureaucrats following advice from government's "law firm" (which is through the justice department in NS) have used this catchphrase to withhold information. There are times when this is legitimate, given the legal consequences that could arise if privilege is waived. But this can also be used as a fallback position when governments don't want to share information that makes them uncomfortable.

While on the subject of keeping things under wraps, we witnessed an increase in the number of discussions that didn't get committed to paper because of the influence of freedom of information laws. There is no question that ministers and cabinets should have and require cabinet confidentiality to do their jobs. But we believe the notion extended to political staff engaged in policy and communications discussions with senior bureaucrats. We took part in some meetings where minutes were not required nor recommended and where verbal direction was articulated by a senior official. In other words, there was nothing in writing providing evidence that a discussion, agreement or recommendation had been made. In some cases, documents handed out in meetings were taken back on our way out of the room. This was done to ensure content would not be leaked or recorded. We often felt uncomfortable and took our own notes, summarized them when we got back to our desk and then electronically transferred them to the person above us or saved them in case we needed ready access to pertinent points if someone called on us to comment or defend ourselves. Yes, it may sound like we were paranoid, but we each had seen enough situations where bureaucrats were thrown under the bus because there was nothing to show that they didn't deserve such treatment.

Unwarranted attacks

Another issue that distorts how the public perceives government actions is the controversy opposition members love to create. Opposition parties constantly attack governments in power. It's part of their job and is ingrained in the party system. The media relish these opportunities. While it's critical to have informed opposition, many times such attacks cloud the issues. Communications suffer as a result. Say a government gets criticized for doing something good; it's unlikely they'll want to attract more controversy. They'll either keep it under wraps the next time or avoid repeating the action.

We will admit to taking some pleasure when an effort to get headlines turned on opposition members who stirred up controversies for controversy's sake. An example that stands out during the early days of our tenure involved an opposition member publicly questioning a former minister of transportation about a line item in the budget. The line item referenced a men's clothing store. The opposition member implied the minister was buying his suits on the government's dime.

It turned out the cost was for highway safety uniforms for employees. Communications employees then had to work to reverse the public's perception that the minister was spending taxpayer dollars on his own suits. This was an unnecessary waste of time and resources. However, it did leave the opposition with egg on their face, which only seemed fair.

Another example involved a program that gave offenders the opportunity to train rescue puppies in partnership with the Nova Scotia SPCA. The opposition claimed that the government was spending $60,000 a year to give prisoners puppies, rightly expecting it would outrage the public at what they described as inappropriate spending of tax dollars. Indeed, headlines blared and radio call-in lines lit up with callers irate over the perceived misuse of their tax dollars. However, when the program was explained — prisoners were training shelter puppies to assist with adoption — many expressed support for the program, and bureaucrats got funding from government to keep the program running. Again, the opposition looked petty and uninformed, but it was the communicators who had to spend time addressing the outrage and reversing the negative perceptions that had been caused.

Resources required to meet diverse information needs

The last stumbling block we'd like to highlight concerns the resources required to develop and share information that responds to citizen needs. Populations are diverse, with resulting language barriers. There is also a need to address the information requirements of members of vulnerable populations, including persons with disabilities, the economically disadvantaged and the elderly. This requires willingness, time, effort and expertise to not only develop materials in a multitude of languages, but also invest in the use of multiple formats and channels to provide the information.

We hope this high-level overview of government communications has left you with a better understanding of the activities bureaucrats undertake to communicate with clients and citizens, as well as the challenges that interfere with delivery. Despite the challenges, government communications are essential and require ongoing effort. Many bureaucrats work hard to share information and keep citizens informed in challenging circumstances.

Case in Point

We wanted to share this paraphrased exchange of email messages to give you a sense of the back-and-forth that can take place just to get permission to issue a news release on a government decision. We hope it provides some insight into why things take longer than expected in the world of communications.

October 5:

First person: I wanted to follow up on our discussion earlier this afternoon. You indicated we could be ready for the 12th with direct communications. We'll need to confirm by next Friday.

Second person: It would be helpful if we could delay for just one more week. We're losing Monday because of Thanksgiving. Thanks very much for following up.

October 12:

First person: Just double checking that we are good to go with next week.

Second person: I think we should make a best effort to get this out the door.

First person: We will need to know by tomorrow morning.

October 13:

Second person: Everyone on this email is offline at the moment. Perhaps we need another week.

October 18:

First person: So, just to confirm: are we waiting until next week?

Third person: Is this now scheduled to move forward next week?

First person: You'll need to confirm this new timeline (it's up to Communications).

Second person: I'm good with the timeline.

October 19:

Fourth person: Could you please confirm that Communications is ready to go?

First person: All is good on our end.

Second person: Staff will post on our website after your press release. Does that work for you?

October 20:

Third person: Please delay communications.

If we lost you as you read through that exchange, we've made our point. We hope you'll have a better appreciation of the hoops that bureaucrats go through to carry out the simplest of communications tasks — in this case, sharing information on a decision that government made.

Our second case concerns a controversial January 2015 news release titled "Lower Seniors' Pharmacare Co-pays Begin Apr. 1," issued by Communications Nova Scotia. The irony of the start date is not lost on us, but the joke was on the government when it had to take back its words. The government was dropping the amount of money people in the program had to pay at the counter from 30 per cent to 20 per cent of the drugs' costs. But the release failed to mention program premiums were jumping from around $500 to $1,200. It's a complicated program, as who pays and who benefits depends on income and medication required in a given year. It's murky and hard to explain in sound bites. The policy position may have been sound — those with more income pay more and those with less pay less, which is a defining principle of living in a social welfare state. However, the debacle culminated with an apology by way of an open letter from the premier to the citizens of NS. Low-income seniors would pay less, but premiums would not go up as announced, and more consultation would take place with seniors. In this case, advocates were organized and vocal.[6]

TALKING POINTS

- Despite the criticisms and missteps, government communications are a critical and necessary function.
- Many bureaucrats work hard to communicate on governments' behalf, with resulting benefits for clients and citizens alike.
- Political considerations can and will influence how government information is shaped and delivered.
- Centralization and automation have not necessarily made for better communications with citizens, nor have they served the institution of government well.
- Being aware of the challenges bureaucrats face when communicating may help the public better appreciate the constraints that hamper interaction.
- The challenges shouldn't stop bureaucrats from trying to communicate, nor stop citizens from listening.
- While it's tempting to want to "shoot the messenger," it's important to recognize that government spokespeople are just delivery agents.
- The field of communications has become increasingly complex, given the myriad of communications channels and the need to adapt information to meet the needs of diverse and vulnerable populations.

Don't take our word for it

We're going to sway from past practice for this section and offer up a response to a question we posed to a former colleague and fellow MPA graduate. Geoff Wilson worked for departments and central communications agencies under various governments, occupying increasingly senior leadership roles. Wilson also did a stint as International Association for Public Participation (IAP2) President.

The question we asked and his response follows While the question and answer are directed to bureaucrats, anybody interested in communicating with or responding to a government can benefit from his insights; this is why we want to share his comments verbatim.

Q: How can bureaucrats work within the confines of central control, gatekeeping and dumbing-down practices to communicate their knowledge and advice on key issues to those who need to hear it? Be that politicians, media or the general public.

A: As renowned Irish playwright George Bernard Shaw famously once said, 'The single biggest problem in communication is the illusion that it has taken place.' In the context of government communications, never have truer words been spoken.

Communicating government policy was never easy at the best of times. In today's world of 24-7 news cycles, social media, citizen journalism and 'fake news' trying to communicate public policy is even harder than ever. On top of this, the public is less trusting of government and traditional media than ever before, opinions are facts (or 'alternative facts'), the attention span of the public is shorter than ever (and competition for the public's attention has become blood-sport), and public policy issues are becoming increasingly more complex.

By this point if you're still reading and not high tailing it to the nearest tavern, you're truly committed to learning how to communicate your policy knowledge and expertise to your political or bureaucracy masters and the public.

Working with the constraints of central control of messaging and communication will be one of the most agonizing and frustrating challenges you will confront. Today, much of centralized government communications has become about government messaging via the news media and social media on key policy initiatives that would stem directly from the governing party's election platform. There are a few exceptions, but the government's primary policy objectives will flow from their promises.

So, the first tip: If your policy advice is not connected to or cannot be framed as part of the government's political agenda, it is probably time to shelve that idea for another day.

Communicators in government and bureaucracy walk the very

fine — and occasionally unhappy — line between government and politics. Make no mistake, however, communications staff take their role as gatekeepers and managers of risk and reputation extremely seriously. No matter how wonderful your policy idea may be, if it puts the minister or government at risk, the communications people will not be shy to say so. In this respect, communications wield a disproportionate amount of formal and informal power within the bureaucracy.

It is also worth noting that communicators often have greater access to political decision makers by virtue of their role, and therefore more opportunities to guide and influence the thinking of politicians and political staff.

The second piece of advice is the same as the first tip: The policy needs to be aligned with the government's political agenda and it must fall within the limits of acceptable political and reputational risk.

Gatekeeping can occur in other ways, such as how governments present policy to the public and how they talk about it. It is probably fair to say that public policy can be complicated if not highly complex, and these are conditions that don't translate well into three bullet point explanations delivered for a 15-second sound bite. Oversimplification of policy through the process of communications packaging is a very real challenge that is no one's fault or intent, but it does challenge the integrity of evidence-based and painstaking policy development processes.

The 24-hour news cycle and information-overload culture we have created pushes us to 'dumb-it-down' by virtue of the medium through which governments have become accustomed to communicating. In this day and age no one has the time or resources to craft carefully planned public information strategies or conduct social marketing campaigns. So, by default there is a media opportunity, a news release or staged media event. These might be backed up with detailed packages, pre-arranged expert interviews, and websites.

We open up a communications buffet and the media consume the free breadsticks and water because they have limited column inches, or just a 60-second spot to fill — and, they may judge that the policy detail simply isn't that interesting or important.

Never forget that news is business, after all.

And so, onto a third piece of advice: You cannot rely on the usual government communications channels to share and promote a policy initiative. In developing the policy if you are not considering how you will share and explain the policy to targeted users outside of a media relations approach, then you are dooming your work to obscurity.

This is not to say that broad-based news media coverage isn't important, rather it cannot be your only strategy.

Through it all, it might seem that government communicators are the enemy of good policy development. That is not at all the message. A good comms person can often help you see your own work through the eyes of the public, and then help you shape the right messages and approaches to bring clarity and understanding or encourage action. Resources, time, creativity, and a public overwhelmed and over-stimulated by information and technology are all realities that push us down a path of expedience — a PR-style event, a clip, the B-roll - that ends with oversimplification of important policy work.

Which brings us around to a fourth and final piece of advice: Communicate policy directly to those most affected by it. Bring them along with you and involve them as much as you can in helping to shape policy. Have them advise you on how best to connect and share the policy with those who will have the greatest need to know.

There is a Chinese proverb which says: 'Tell me, I forget. Show me, I remember. Involve me, I understand.' Public policy communication in today's world needs to transcend the communications practices from the mass media/mass communications age.

The world has moved beyond that. People have unlimited choice in what information they can consume, and when and how they consume it.

And, no offence, your policy work isn't competing with the latest Instagram sensation.

If you take steps to involve users and stakeholders in fashioning policy from the outset, the communications effort will be accomplished before the policy is even ready to become the subject of a news release from communications central.

It may not surprise you to learn, that a secondary outcome will be better policy and greater trust in government.

To bring this all back to the beginning, and Mr. Bernard Shaw's erudite observation about communications: Don't create the illusion of communication of important public policy work by giving in to singular communication approaches. Engage others in the work. Bring them along with you. Forge stronger, more trusting connections with those for whom the policy will have the greatest influence and impact by having them help shape the policy and its implementation. Make it familiar to them so they can embrace it.

Conclusion

THAT'S A WRAP

Thank you for taking this journey through the landscape of bureaucracy with us.

Our purpose in writing this book was to share the voice of the bureaucrat; a voice that is seldom heard in discussions about government.

By giving you our bureaucrat's playbook, we hope we've helped to build some empathy regarding the challenges bureaucrats face while working in a politically charged environment.

We tried to paint a picture that depicts the breadth and scope of the work bureaucrats throughout the country undertake on behalf of citizens, including how they navigate plenty of rocky terrain. Contrary to stereotypes and negative perceptions, within the bureaucracy, there is a talent pool of educated, ethical, professional, creative, dedicated and highly specialized people.

We're thankful for the role these people play on a daily basis, especially when society faces significant threats like the 2020 COVID-19 pandemic. COVID-19 was a major marker in the course of world health, economics and citizenship. The strengths and weaknesses of public systems were put to the test in ways we never imagined. In some circles, public servants were hailed for their efforts to rise to the occasion, including demonstrating their ability to take risks. It is our hope that bureaucracies founded on the principles we've outlined stand the test of time. We hope the lessons we shared shape the way those critical societal tasks are carried out in the future.

We valued our careers as bureaucrats and we're especially proud of this book, as we believe we're still serving the public good by challenging the stereotypes; making it easier for anybody trying to navigate the bureaucracy; inspiring those currently serving to keep up their good work; and encouraging others to join the service.

ACKNOWLEDGEMENTS

We end this book with a shout out to all the people who encouraged and supported this work. They include some key informants, who are referenced in this book, including: Jim Baker, Sharon Davis-Murdoch, Geoff D'Eon, Bruce Hennebury, Fred Honsberger, Doug Keefe, Gregory Keefe, Charlie Macdonald, Ray MacNeil, Rosalind Penfound, Tilly Pillay and Geoff Wilson. We also want to thank our first readers also, including: Patti Pike, John Campbell and Karen Fitzner, as well as our early supporters: Ramon Baltazar, Jocyeln Bourgon and Laura Lee Langley. And we are grateful to the team at Formac Publishing for their guidance and sage advice.

Appendix A
TYPICAL LIFE STAGES OF A BUREAUCRAT

The following is our take on the typical life stages of a bureaucrat and what to expect while going through each one. Much of this stems from our own experiences; we recognize that everyone has their own story. Having said that, we thought it may help prepare readers on what to expect if they are considering a career as a bureaucrat or are currently in this role and wondering what they may expect in the future.

We're starting this exploration with some thoughts on why people want to join the civil service.

Many may be looking for stable, secure jobs. Others may want the benefit package they believe exists, while some have been moved in that direction because some family members were life-long civil servants. We did not witness a shift in the reasons why people wanted to join over the years; rather, we met more and more who wanted to make their communities better and thought becoming a bureaucrat was a good way to do that. People entering the public service today tend to have more formal education, are more knowledgeable about the issues facing government and are better prepared to navigate the systems of their workplace. Many have post-secondary education or other highly developed skills, which is a relatively new phenomenon.

Roles and Job Prospects

There are lots of job prospects in government. An observation from a 2014 *Globe and Mail* article reported that jobs "can range from overseeing budgets to managing government programs in areas such as health, education, transportation or finance. Depending on what position or level of government, the job can be specific to one sector or across the board."[1]

Entry Point

Journeys to enter the public service usually begin with an online job search of government postings. The position postings describe the role, the duties and responsibilities, the qualifications, the classification and the salary. This is likely the first time some people realize government speaks a different language; they will find many buzzwords and acronyms throughout the posting. It's also likely some job duties will leave readers more confused than ever about what their actual work involves. Even the titles of the positions can leave people scratching their heads. Consider this one from a Nova Scotia government posting for a "Strategist, Issues Management" reporting to the "Managing Director, Operations Leadership, Coordination and Alignment Branch of the Department of Business," with a salary as high as $92,000. We expect those outside of government, and many who are working in the system, have no idea what the person in this role will do, why it warrants such a good salary and how it contributes to creating a better society for Nova Scotians.

Postings may also be the first exposure people have to union rules. The rules can turn people off from applying because the vast majority of union positions are open to union members first.

Getting screened in is probably the most difficult part of this process. In our time, there was an unwritten rule that suggests hiring managers interview between three and five people. It is a reasonable number, but narrowing the field to such a small selection of hopeful candidates makes it difficult for people to land a spot when hundreds of applications are received for each role.

The interview is the next hurdle for those who make it through the screening process. Like most large institutions, public sector organizations have a fairly rigid interview process. It likely includes a panel interview of at least three interviewers, who will invite applicants into a small boardroom — generally windowless — and ask scripted questions, rating the answers based on how well they match the panel's preferred responses. Candidates will want to make sure they have done some homework, including reading business plans and accountability reports (usually available online), so they can speak to the challenges of the department and the competencies deemed critical for the role. They'll also want to keep their answers within an hour. This is the time typically allotted for each candidate, and we have seen plenty of situations where people did not earn any favours for going beyond the allotted time. Like any organization, those from inside are expected to have an upper hand; they know the nuances of the organization, what the leaders are looking for and can cite examples of typical scenarios that directly apply to the work setting.

Next is waiting to hear whether one got the job, which could take only a week or stretch into a month or two. The time spent waiting depends on the levels of authority that have to sign off on the candidate. For a relatively junior position, several signatures will be required. Those who need to sign off are presumably busy; approval paperwork can sit on a desk for days before moving on to the next person. We have witnessed situations where the preferred candidate was no longer on the market by the time the offer was made.

Negotiating Terms on Their Terms

Many people preparing for job interviews spend time thinking about how to negotiate their terms of employment. For the most part, people applying for government positions can skip over this part of preparation. Like many systems within the bureaucracy, rigid rules and policies dictate how things play out; this includes employment terms. For a fairly senior role, there may be some wiggle room for extra vacation entitlement and salary, but the majority of new hires will be notified of their salary and benefits, and that will be that.

The *Globe and Mail* article referenced earlier noted "salaries start at about $45,000 for entry-level positions, but can increase dramatically, depending on the role and level of experience, to more than $300,000 for workers at the highest levels in the public service."[2] We can tell you those higher-end salaries are few and far between.

First Day on the Job

New hires can expect to be presented with a ton of paper or online links to keep them occupied during that first day. Chances are those in specialized positions will hit the ground running. However, staff in new administrative positions in a head office environment may find themselves stuck reading documents for a few weeks, waiting for their boss to explain what is expected of them. New bureaucrats should enjoy the downtime; when they are finally given their marching orders, they're going to long for those early days.

We're concluding this section with a tip from Glenda Eoyang, a pioneer in the applications of complexity science to human and organizational systems, who shared three simple rules to navigate any organization or situation. These include flying toward the centre of the flock, matching the speed of others and avoiding bumping into anybody or anything.[3]

Command Performance

If the performance management process is followed correctly, bureaucrats should have specific annual goals and development plans and most will diligently work to achieve and surpass those goals. Unfortunately, during our time in government, most new employees were not given goals or objectives when they started. Leading up to their annual performance review, they were told to work backwards and identify the goals that matched the work they completed. This wasn't a great first impression of the process and created a great deal of cynicism regarding performance management.

Unless there has been a performance issue, a bureaucrat will likely meet with their boss at the end of the year and give examples of how they met or exceeded their goals, what training they had to help them and how they think they did overall.

During our time, the performance scale went from one to five; the number rating was critical because it tied into bonuses. Those receiving a one or two got nothing; a three often meant a 1 per cent raise and a four or a five could have translated into a 2–4 per cent increase.

Here is where things often went wrong. There were several instances wherein employees who exceeded their stated goals were given a "solid three" only because they had been given a four the previous year. They were well-deserving of the four in the second year, but yes, the bell curve came into play, a common practice in many organizations outside of the public sector. This was so prevalent when we were working, a refrain among many was to "be all you can be, be a three." As for impact, many people stopped trying to be "the best." Don't get us wrong — these same people gave a solid performance and did their job well, but imagine what could have been accomplished if everyone truly strived, and was recognized for, a stellar performance.

One of us was told that although expectations in terms of responsibility and action were exceeded, the boss could not capture that on paper. A rating of four would not be assigned as the department was told there could only be so many fours, given resources available. This was especially discouraging for someone who had always achieved an outstanding rating and was motivated by positive feedback.

We're concluding this section with an observation on performance evaluations complements of Sarah Knight in *The Life-changing Magic of Not Giving a F*ck*: "You probably have to show up to your performance evaluation if you want to keep your job. But — and I know this may sound counterintuitive — you don't have to give a f*ck about it while you're sitting there. Why? Because this is a situation in which the die has been cast. That evaluation has already been rendered by your boss; today just happens to be the day you have to listen to it."[4]

Looking for Praise in All the Wrong Places

We think public sector employees attach importance to the intrinsic value of their work and are less motivated by monetary rewards. Thankfully, that's the case, because there are limits on what managers can do to reward employees. This is, in part, due to public opinion and the refrain that taxpayers pay government employee salaries. Many people believe that bureaucrats are already paid too much and loudly voice their opinions that a cent more for anything is a cent too much.

Employees may also want to look for ways to thank their colleagues and to feel proud about the great work they do without that external pat on the back, because chances are it won't be forthcoming. It is also highly unlikely they will get many thanks from the public or politicians.

Of course, there are the obligatory ceremonial recognition awards, such as long service. These awards are significant for some employees. Those working in the field may have never met a senior official, minister or premier; being face-to-face with them is exciting and rewarding. Others may view the awards as insincere glad-handing by politicians. If ministers were grateful for all the hard work bureaucrats did on their behalf, one would think it would be easy to get them to attend. Sadly, in our experience, it was much easier to get the opposition members to show up to these ceremonies than our elected leaders.

Upward Mobility

The promotion process is much like the hiring process: bureaucrats see an opportunity and apply. However, be warned. During our years of service, some positions were posted, but we already knew, as did everybody else on the inside, who was to be promoted. It's not unusual for people to have favourites.

If bureaucrats do take on senior responsibilities, they may want to prepare to feel isolated. There is lots of talk about mentorship and peer collegiality, but we didn't witness much of this. People were too busy treading water to help others from drowning. One of our former deputies said it was the loneliest job she had ever had.

Lack of succession management was also an issue. We heard those words bandied about for years. Ultimately, union rules limit how government can move employees around to help them get the experience necessary for promotion. It is difficult to recruit and promote new employees when time served overrides merit.

We recall one senior leader declaring that "succession management is the biggest oxymoron I've ever heard." She was frustrated; she was expected to put in hours of work assessing, mentoring and educating employees who were seen as high potentials, when she knew that, at the end of the day, she would have to go through a process that didn't ensure anyone she spent time developing would be promoted. We heard this complaint from many.

The above frustration for this leader was due to the fair hiring policy. While it is sound policy, it does inhibit the ability to appoint people who have been groomed for promotion. To live up to the policy, managers can't cherry-pick who they want to promote without a competition.

And on the mobility front, should bureaucrats be tempted to take on a political role, they should be aware that it is difficult to turn back. They will want to be confident the party they've chosen has a long tenure. At the heart of the matter, non-partisanship will be questioned, and bureaucrats could lose civil servant status. Unfortunately, if they were in a union, that protection will be gone as well.

Special Project Officers ... Always Say No

Our last piece of advice on the upward mobility track is this: bureaucrats should avoid taking on jobs with a "special project officer" title if they're in for the long haul. In our experience, these positions were reserved predominately for senior civil servants who had managed to somehow slight or annoy a deputy or political figure. It was usually a transition role that led straight out the door to an early retirement or unplanned departure. Bureaucrats beware: if someone is offering up such a role, they should keep their back to the wall.

Check Out/Retirement

Those lucky enough to reach the magic formula, which was a sum of 80 (age plus years of service; this has since jumped to 85) can retire without penalty. Many do. It is a fairly streamlined process, where bureaucrats submit their forms to human resources and the pension agency. They then enjoy or endure the typical public servant retiree gathering, consisting of coffee and sweets in the boardroom and attended by one or two senior members who were provided with speaking notes. It can be an easy transition for many with a sense of relief and pride at this end to their years of service. For others, it can be a time filled with angst and resentment. We knew people who carried resentment because they left without seeing abusive supervisors called out and required to change their ways. And there were other passionate, well-meaning employees who saw too much time wasted, bad decisions made and intolerance that can be found in every department.

Either way, the employee is off to a whole new world. Or are they? In far too many instances, employees have used their retirement as part of their financial plan. Take an employee who meets the sum of 85 and decides they will retire, but remain as a casual or a contract employee. While some may agree this is a smart move for the employee, it leaves a bad taste in the mouth for many others. One grievance, as such, is that this individual is now on the retirement payroll and is double-dipping into another payment. They are making on average 1.5 times what the pay for that position warrants. The practice also prohibits existing employees from getting promotions and reduces opportunities for new employees to get into the system. Think of an old growth forest and the natural cycle of replenishment. In this case, such practices limit knowledge transfer and the injection of new talent and can be demoralizing for those who have to witness it.

Before we left, changes were made to pension rules that made this practice less attractive. For example, after six months, the employee had to start paying into the pension plan again. But, like most rules, people found ways to get around them, working in five-month periods and taking short breaks in between or working on a personal services contract.

One last note regarding retirees: some know they'll be retiring in a few years and immediately start the process of mentally checking out from their responsibilities as a civil service worker. This is unfortunate. If, perhaps, you are one of them, we hope our book provides some inspiration to continue working for the public good.

Appendix B

THE BUREAUCRAT'S LEXICON

To help inject some humour as we went about our daily chores, we came up with our own definitions for overused words in the government workplace. Here is our take on the more prominent ones:

Agenda: everybody has one, including you

Alignment: used manipulatively to get your pet project approved

Best practice: used to refer to your personal favourites on how things should be done

Champion: often used to inflate someone's ego

Collaborate: making nice with others when you have no choice

Consensus: not to be confused with truth

Continuous improvement: what governments fail to do because they are too busy thinking strategically

Dialogue: another overused term used to prolong decision making

Doing more with less: this is impossible to achieve, despite what the "champions" say; it also suggests we're not focused on priorities

Dynamic: used to describe something that isn't

Election cycle: yes, yes, yes, no, no, no, maybe, maybe, maybe and back to yes, yes, yes

Empowerment: a term that creates a visceral reaction because it is used disingenuously

Evidence-based decision making: an ideal that has been corrupted into decision-based evidence making

Feasibility: as in "explore the feasibility," which is bureaucratic cover for delaying a decision

Framework: a living document to help guide initiatives and actions of multiple players

High-level review: a bureaucrat has done a quick scan of the issue

In the fullness of time; in due time: as in, we will not get back to you

Initiative: an idea that isn't going anywhere, according to comedian George Carlin[1]

Innovation: used repeatedly and for anything

Investment: another word for corporate welfare

Lens: something that is supposed to make things clearer, but actually clouds the issues

Moving forward: as in two steps forward, three steps back

Question period: don't expect answers; it's called question period, after all

Quick win: a minister's dream because these are "announceables"

Shared priority: another way to say pass the buck

Silly season: the period leading up to the election when anything and nothing goes

Strategy: developed when there is no money to actually do things; used "strategically" as a delay tactic

Streamline: another overused term suggesting inefficiency

Transformational: another impossible goal, as government is by its very nature meant to be stable

Transparency: a utopian state that will never be reached

ENDNOTES

INTRODUCTION

1. Jay Makarenko, "Provincial Government in Canada: Organization, Institutions & Issues," (Mar. 4, 2009), https://www.mapleleafweb.com/features/provincial-government-canada-organization-institutions-issues.html.

CHAPTER 1

1. International Churchill Society, https://winstonchurchill.org/resources/quotes/the-worst-form-of-government.
2. Makarenko, "Provincial Government in Canada: Organization, Institutions & Issues."
3. Ibid.
4. "Political Jobs in Ottawa: Legislative Assistants (LAs) to Members of Parliament," https://www2.mystfx.ca/sites/mystfx.ca.political-science/files/gmglareport.pdf.
5. Michal Gorman, "Court documents allege premier, others knew of plan for 'unconquered people' argument," *CBC News* (Feb. 20, 2020), https://www.cbc.ca/news/canada/nova-scotia/alex-cameron-nova-scotia-justice-department-affidavit-conquered-peoples-1.5469939.
6. Haley Ryan, "Province says 'unconquered people' lawyer was repeatedly told to abandon argument," *CBC News* (Jul. 16, 2020), https://www.cbc.ca/news/canada/nova-scotia/nova-scotia-defence-lawsuit-defamation-lawyer-alton-gas-1.5652041.
7. Peter Aucoin, "New Political Governance in Westminster Systems: Impartial Public Administration and Management Performance at Risk," *Governance: An International Journal of Policy, Administration, and Institutions*, Vol. 25, No. 2 (April 2012), © 2012 Wiley Periodicals, Inc. https://onlinelibrary.wiley.com/doi/full/10.1111/j.1468-0491.2012.01569.x.

CHAPTER 2

1. Statement from the Minister, Finance and Treasury Board, Province of Nova Scotia (August 19, 2015), https://novascotia.ca/news/release/?id=20150819001.
2. Tim Bousquet, "Bullshitter of the Summer: Randy Delorey." Morning File, *Halifax Examiner* (Aug. 19, 2015), https://www.halifaxexaminer.ca/featured/bullshitter-of-the-summer-randy-delorey-morning-file-wednesday-august-19-2015.
3. Jesse Snyder, "Liberals to hike pay for 10,000 bureaucrats even as federal deficit continues to swell," *National Post* (Jul. 22, 2020), https://nationalpost.com/news/liberals-to-hike-pay-for-10000-bureaucrats-even-as-federal-deficit-continues-to-swell.
4. Michal Gorman, "Stephen McNeil says Marilla Stephenson got no special treatment," *CBC News* (Jul. 25, 2016), https://www.cbc.ca/news/canada/nova-scotia/stephen-mcneil-nsgeu-marilla-stephenson-1.3693558.
5. Michael Gorman, "Public Service Commission got job input from applicant who was eventually hired," *CBC News* (Jul. 24, 2016), https://www.cbc.ca/news/canada/nova-scotia/premier-job-description-marilla-stephenson-1.3693092.
6. "Glennie Langille given patronage appointment by Liberals," *CBC News* (Dec. 3, 2013), https://www.cbc.ca/news/canada/nova-scotia/glennie-langille-given-patronage-appointment-by-liberals-1.2449356.
7. Jean Laroche, "Job McNeil once described as patronage post moves to civil service," *CBC News*, (Oct. 31, 2018), https://www.cbc.ca/news/canada/nova-scotia/glennie-langille-protocol-office-politics-patronage-1.4885695.

8. Government of Canada, Canada School of Public Service, https://www.csps-efpc.gc.ca/index-eng.aspx.
9. SNC-Lavalin Affairs, Wikipedia, https://en.wikipedia.org/wiki/SNC-Lavalin_affair.
10. James Comey, *A Higher Loyalty: Truth, Lies, and Leadership* (Macmillan Publishers' Flatiron Books: April 2018).
11. Patricia W. Ingraham and Nadia Rubaii-Barrett, "Human Resource Management as a Core Dimension of Public Administration," *The Foundations of Public Administration Series*, https://faculty.cbpp.uaa.alaska.edu/afgjp/PADM601%20Fall%202009/FPA-HRM-Article.pdf.
12. John Paul Tasker, "Public service video featuring only white bureaucrats sends 'the wrong message': minister," *CBC News* (Jun. 22, 2020), https://www.cbc.ca/news/politics/public-service-all-white-bureaucrats-video-1.5622772.
13. Christopher Chabris and Daniel Simons, *The Invisible Gorilla*, http://theinvisiblegorilla.com/gorilla_experiment.html.
14. Andrew Duffy, "Canada's civil service is world's most effective: UK report," *Ottawa Citizen*, (Jul. 10, 2017), https://ottawacitizen.com/news/local-news/canadas-civil-service-is-worlds-most-effective-uk-report.

CHAPTER 3
1. Aucoin, "New Political Governance in Westminster Systems: Impartial Public Administration and Management Performance at Risk."

CHAPTER 4
1. Jim Vibert, "Shift report is PR poorly done," *The Chronicle Herald* (Dec. 19, 2018), https://www.thechronicleherald.ca/opinion/vibert-shift-report-is-pr-poorly-done-269572.
2. Donald J. Savoie, *What Is Government Good At? A Canadian Answer* (McGill-Queen's University Press: September, 2015), https://www.mqup.ca/what-is-government-good-at--products-9780773546219.php.
3. John Buntin, "25 Years Later, What Happened to 'Reinventing Government'?" (September 2016), https://www.governing.com/topics/mgmt/gov-reinventing-government-book.html.
4. "Delivery man", *The Economist* (March 2015), https://www.economist.com/books-and-arts/2015/03/26/delivery-man.
5. Rex Murphy, "Deliverology, where are thy successes?" *National Post* (Oct. 6, 2017), https://nationalpost.com/opinion/rex-murphy-deliverology-where-are-thy-successes.
6. "Obliquity," John Kay, January 17, 2004; https://www.johnkay.com/2004/01/17/obliquity.
7. Jerry Z. Muller, *The Tyranny of Metrics* (Princeton University Press: 2018), https://press.princeton.edu/books/paperback/9780691191911/the-tyranny-of-metrics.
8. Andrea Jones-Rooy, "I'm a data scientist who is skeptical about data" *Quartz* (July 2019), https://qz.com/1664575/is-data-science-legit.
9. Sarah Knight, *The Life-changing Magic of Not Giving a F*ck* (Little, Brown and Company: 2015).

CHAPTER 5
1. "100 Management Guide — Forms", Nova Scotia Government, Executive Council Office, https://novascotia.ca/treasuryboard/manuals/100forms.htm.
2. "Executive Council Submissions Handbook," Northwest Territories (January 2014), https://www.eia.gov.nt.ca/sites/eia/files/2018_12_13_ecshb.pdf.
3. Government of Canada, Memoranda to Cabinet, https://www.canada.ca/en/privy-council/services/publications/memoranda-cabinet.html.
4. "A Guide to Policy Development," Office of the Auditor General, Manitoba, https://www.oag.mb.ca/wp-content/uploads/2019/10/PolicyDevelopmentGuide.pdf.
5. Graham Steele, "Citizens' Guide to the Nova Scotia Legislature," https://grahamsteeleblog.wordpress.com/2016/12/09/q3-what-is-the-process-to-make-a-law.
6. Makarenko, "Provincial Government in Canada: Organization, Institutions & Issues."
7. "An Introduction to how Canada's Parliament works", Parliament of Canada, https://lop.parl.ca/about/parliament/education/ourcountryourparliament/html_booklet/process-passing-bill-e.html.

8.   "How an Ontario Bill Becomes Law — a guide for legislators and the public," Legislative Research Service, Legislative Assembly of Ontario (August 2011), https://www.ola.org/sites/default/files/common/how-bills-become-law-en.pdf.

9.   Paul Withers, "Some Trudeau government ocean initiatives greeted with skepticism in Halifax," *CBC News* (Jan. 16, 2020), https://www.cbc.ca/news/canada/nova-scotia/trudeau-government-ocean-initiatives-scepticism-1.5428741?ref=mobilerss&cmp=newsletter_CBC%20Nova%20Scotia_193_591.

10. "Business Plan 2019–20," Department of Fisheries and Aquaculture, Government of Nova Scotia, https://novascotia.ca/government/accountability/2019-2020/2019-2020-business-plan-Department-of-Fisheries-and-Aquaculture.pdf.

11. Aucoin, "New Political Governance in Westminster Systems: Impartial Public Administration and Management Performance at Risk."

CHAPTER 6

1.   Ida Bae Wells, @nhannahjones, https://twitter.com/nhannahjones/status/1244797223973552131?lang=en.

2.   Ali Farazmand, ed., *Privatization or Public Enterprise Reform? International Case Studies with Implications for Public Management*, in *Contributions in Economics and Economic History*, Number 220 (Greenwood Press: 2001), https://books.google.ca/books?id=ZRaLRcatOScC&printsec=frontcover#v=onepage&q&f=false.

3.   We've paraphrased these descriptions from material we found online, and you can find the source here: https://kaninzi.com/wp-content/uploads/2018/06/TypesOfEvaluation.pdf.

4.   Emma Smith, "Health authority anticipated blowback after cutting online prenatal classes," *CBC News* (Apr. 3, 2019), https://www.cbc.ca/news/canada/nova-scotia/prenatal-classes-nova-scotia.

5.   Emma Smith, "N.S. moms question province's decision to scrap online prenatal classes," *CBC News* (Jan. 26, 2019), https://www.cbc.ca/news/canada/nova-scotia/prenatal-education-health-parents-online-class-welcome-to-parenting-1.4992839.

6.   Smith, "Health authority anticipated blowback after cutting online prenatal classes."

7.   Christian Bason, "For more efficient government, don't start with efficiency," Centre for Public Impact (Jan. 22, 2019), https://www.centreforpublicimpact.org/for-more-efficient-government-dont-start-with-efficiency-in-conversation-with-christian-bason.

CHAPTER 7

1.   Paul Bennett, "The Savage Revolution: A perilous experiment in reinventing government," *The Chronicle Herald* (December 4, 2017), D4.

2.   Donald J. Savoie, *Whatever Happened to the Music Teacher? How Government Decides and Why*, (McGill-Queen's University Press: 2013), https://www.mqup.ca/whatever-happened-to-the-music-teacher--products-9780773541108.php#!.

3.   Canadian Intergovernmental Conference Secretariat, https://scics.ca/en/organization-overview.

4.   Savoie, *Whatever Happened to the Music Teacher? How Government Decides and Why.*

CHAPTER 8

1.   Government of Canada, Open Government, https://open.canada.ca/en.

2.   Nova Scotia Government's Open Data Portal, https://data.novascotia.ca.

3.   Ontario Government Data Catalogue: https://data.ontario.ca.

4.   "18th Annual Report on Government of Canada Public Opinion Research Activities," Government of Canada, Minister of Public Works and Government Services (2019), https://www.tpsgc-pwgsc.gc.ca/rop-por/rapports-reports/documents/rapport-report-2018-2019-new-eng.pdf.

5.   "Strengthening Public Engagement, Op-ed", Nova Scotia Treasury Board (May 13, 2011), https://novascotia.ca/news/release/?id=20110513001.

6.   "Voluntary Planning: So much for openness," editorial in *The Chronicle Herald* (May 2011).

7.   Bill Tieleman, "Canadian Taxpayers Federation Demands Accountability, but Not for Itself," *The Tyee* (Sep 17, 2013), https://thetyee.ca/Opinion/2013/09/17/Canadian-Taxpayers-Federation-Accountability.

8.   Shari Graydon, "Matter. Of. Fact. If only government decisions were …", Special to the *Globe and*

Mail (September 13, 2010), https://www.theglobeandmail.com/opinion/matter-of-fact-if-only-government-decisions-were/article1213488.

9.   Twila Reid, "The moon is innocent and 'Because it's 2015,'" *Canadian Lawyer Magazine* (November 9, 2015), https://www.canadianlawyermag.com/news/general/the-moon-is-innocent-and-because-its-2015/269972.

10.   Toby Mendell, "Guess whose access laws are more open than Nova Scotia's?" (June 14, 2010), http://www.law-democracy.org/wp-content/uploads/2010/09/Guess-whose-access-laws-are-more-open-than-Nova-Scotia's.pdf.

11.   "22 Minutes blasts past the 'Doris' mark," *CBC News* (Nov 18, 2000), https://www.cbc.ca/news/canada/22-minutes-blasts-past-the-doris-mark-1.210915.

12.   Our Luther King, https://ourlutherking.com/martin-luther-king-jr-quotes-on-education.

13.   Andrea Jones-Rooy, "I'm a data scientist who is skeptical about data," *Quartz* (July 2019), https://qz.com/1664575/is-data-science-legit.

CHAPTER 9

1.   Alex Marland, "Strategic Management of Media Relations: Communications Centralization and Spin in the Government of Canada", *Canadian Public Policy*, Volume 43 Issue 1 (March 2017), https://www.utpjournals.press/doi/full/10.3138/cpp.2016-037.

2.   Ibid.

3.   Ibid.

4.   Aucoin, "New Political Governance in Westminster Systems: Impartial Public Administration and Management Performance at Risk."

5.   Philip Cross, "Canada's civil service has forgotten it's supposed to serve 'us,'" Special to *Financial Post* (Oct 23, 2018), https://financialpost.com/opinion/philip-cross-canadas-civil-service-has-forgotten-its-supposed-to-serve-us.

6.   "Lower Seniors' Pharmacare Co-pays Begin April," Health and Wellness, Province of Nova Scotia, January 15, 2016, https://novascotia.ca/news/release/?id=20160115003.

APPENDIX A

1.   Brenda Bouw, "I want to work in the public sector. What will my salary be?" Special to the *Globe and Mail* (February 12, 2014), https://www.theglobeandmail.com/report-on-business/careers/career-advice/life-at-work/i-want-to-work-in-the-public-sector-what-will-my-salary-be/article16834738.

2.   Ibid.

3.   Glenda Eoyang, "Simple Rules: See, Understand, and Influence Patterns," Human Systems Dynamics Institute (2014), http://s3.amazonaws.com/hsd.herokuapp.com/contents/237/original/Simple_Rules_LVW_06Nov14.pdf?1415382443.

4.   Sarah Knight, *The Life-changing Magic of Not Giving a F*ck.*

APPENDIX B

1.   https://learningenglish.voanews.com/a/a-23-2008-07-09-voa3-83136517/117421.html.

INDEX